Managing Your Career in a Downturn

Harvard Business Press

Boston, Massachusetts

Content in this book was previously published in *Shaping Your Career, Managing Stress*, and *Managing Time* © Harvard Business School Publishing, 2006–2008

Library of Congress Cataloging-in-Publication Data
Managing your career in a downturn.
    p. cm.
 ISBN 978-1-4221-2966-1 (pbk.)
1. Career development. 2. Time management. 3. Stress management. I. Harvard Business School. Press.
 HF5381.M2865 2009
 650.14—dc22

                    2009010481

The paper used in this publication meets the requirements of the American National Standard for Permanence of Paper for Publications and Documents in Libraries and Archives Z39.48-1992.

Contents

Part II: Managing Stress 57

Part III: Managing Time 125

Introduction

In a downturn, a company thinks carefully and strategically about its positioning in its industry and the value of its products and services. This strategic focus helps it remain competitive and profitable. Likewise, in a downturn it is particularly critical that you think about your position within your organization and the value of your skills and interests. "Why?" you might ask, "It's not like I'm going to get promoted in this kind of economic environment anyway." But by constantly clarifying what you want to learn next and then taking the steps to obtain that knowledge, you become increasingly valuable to your company. You also stand an excellent chance of finding renewed satisfaction in your work, and you'll be on great footing as the downturn ends.

All of this takes time and some extensive inquiry into who you are and what kinds of work you find most stimulating. In Part I of this guide, "Shaping Your Career," you'll find a wealth of suggestions and strategies for managing that process.

But you know it's not that easy; especially during a downturn it can be hard enough just to get your job done. Does this sound familiar? It's 7:30 on a Friday night, and you're still at your desk after a long, stressful week in the office. Earlier this week, one of your best employees gave notice. Rumors of a layoff have started circulating around the company. Since your spouse was laid off, it's been hard to make ends meet. And two hours ago, your boss piled yet another project on your plate—one that you usually would have pushed back on, but with the layoff rumor. . .well, you just have to get it done. The project you *want* to do keeps getting buried deeper in your inbox. You're definitely feeling the adrenaline coursing through your system.

"Come on," you tell yourself, "Life is always going to be filled with stressful situations. Just ignore it; it'll go away."

You're right that life will always present stress. However, a word of caution about trying to ignore it. If you let your stress level soar too high—and stay that way for too long—you, your team, and your company could pay a high price. Sustained, toxic stress can hurt your health and your performance on the job, preventing you from managing your team effectively, which in turn makes it difficult for the team to function at an optimal level. Managing your stress levels is a key part of managing yourself and your career in a downturn.

In Part II, "Managing Stress," you'll learn to look at and manage stress itself. You'll learn how to recognize what kinds of stress are actually good for you, how to assess your stress level, and how to counteract bad stress with easy-to-use methods.

Another aspect to managing stress is managing your time well. Everyone seems to be frustrated with not having enough time— feeling like we're not getting done what we think we should, or that we have lost control. When it's hard to say no to that extra project because layoffs are always at the back of your mind, you need to find a way to prioritize your work. In Part III, "Managing Time," you'll learn the skills you need to allocate your time wisely and then discipline yourself to keep to your plan. You'll learn to leverage your time to get the most out of your day and execute your job more effectively.

Making the effort to shape your career in a downturn will pay big dividends: you boost your chances of deriving immense satisfaction from your work as well as making your best possible contribution to your organization.

Shaping Your Career

What Does Shaping Your Career Mean?

T HE PROCESS OF assessing where you are in your work life, deciding where you want to be, and then making the changes necessary to get there is called *shaping your career*. It's an ongoing process that *you* orchestrate and that you must manage, thanks to important changes in the business arena.

Understanding the need for change

The world is changing fast, including the world of work. The increasing pace of change that has marked recent decades can leave you breathless sometimes, whether you're a manager in a large corporation, an entrepreneur running your own business, an individual contributor in a small company, or an independent contractor providing services to clients.

When it comes to your career, change is natural—and it's healthy! You strengthen your professional abilities every time you take on new challenges, gain insight into what you want from your work, and learn a new set of skills. You then find more satisfaction in your work *and* contribute more to your organization.

Growing at your company

As you think about redefining your career path (or discovering a new one), take care that you don't fall victim to the all-too-common migration temptation—the belief that if you're unhappy in your job, you should go to another company. The fact is that it may not be your *company* that's the problem. More likely, it's something about your current *role*.

You stand an excellent chance of finding renewed satisfaction in your work if you take advantage of opportunities at your company that match best with your interests, by either enhancing your current role or taking on one or more entirely new roles within the firm. Your company benefits, too, because it now has an even more loyal employee (you!), without incurring the costs of evaluating, hiring, and training someone to replace you.

Organizations large and small now realize that, in order to remain competitive in a fast-changing world, they need employees who:

- Are dedicated to the idea of continuous learning

- Regularly assess their interests, values, and skills so as to figure out the kinds of work for which they are best suited

- Are committed to their company's success

- Understand the skills and behaviors the company will need in the future—and are willing and able to respond quickly and flexibly to develop those capabilities

- Can move easily across functional boundaries and between regular duties and special projects

What Would YOU Do?

Old Dog, New Tricks?

AVID HAD AN epiphany: He didn't want to work in advertising anymore. He liked the people, but he was realizing that he no longer found his career stimulating. Then reality set in. He thought to himself: "I'm too old to start from scratch. Too old to learn new skills. And too old to go back to school."

Yet David realized that he had years of valuable knowledge and experience. Everyone said he was a great manager, and he had a knack for understanding client needs.

Then it hit him. "I'm *not* too old to start something new—I'm too young to give up on my dreams!" But where should he start? What should he do to start moving himself in the right direction?

What would YOU do? See *What You COULD Do*.

Navigating the job-change process

Even though change is natural and healthy, that doesn't mean it's always easy. Managing your own professional development entails some focused effort on your part. First (and most critical), you have to know yourself. Knowing yourself means that you can articulate how the following categories apply to you.

- Your most passionate *business interests* are the kinds of work you're most passionate about.

- Your deepest *work values* are the rewards—such as autonomy, money, close working relationships with colleagues—that you consider most important.

- Your strongest *skills* are your abilities, the things you have learned how to do, such as use a spreadsheet program for data analysis.

Second, you need to become familiar with the many different development opportunities and resources your company has to offer. And third, you pursue those opportunities that you've identified are best for you.

This process can be both exciting and daunting. Prepare to feel stuck at times and to feel that things are moving way too fast at other times. The good news is that many resources are available to help you through the career growth process—including support and insight from your colleagues, friends, and family. You can also take advantage of a selection of formal assessment tools to help you clarify your interests, values, and skills.

If you know what to expect ahead of time, you'll be better able to navigate the change process.

What You COULD Do.

Remember David's desire for change in his career in advertising?

As David begins the process of thinking about a new career, he might ask himself the following questions:

- What are his core business interests—that is, what types of work is he most passionate about? For example, does he prefer problem solving, working with people, or making decisions?
- What are his deepest work values? For example, does he care more about having autonomy or earning a big salary?
- What are his strongest skills?

Once he has identified the answers to these questions, he will be on his way to defining and navigating a new career path or a new direction within the career he's currently in.

Taking Charge
of Your Career

I N TODAY'S BUSINESS environment, the "contract" between employer and employee no longer exists in many companies. So it's up to you to continually define and direct your own career.

Defining your career

The idea that employees should be in charge of their own professional development is relatively new. In the past, people expected to choose a career early in life, find an employer, and then stay at that company for the rest of their working lives. The company was the plane, its leaders were the pilots, and the employees were the passengers. Today, everyone is a pilot.

In the past, in return for their loyalty and longevity at the company, employees received all sorts of protections—including job security, a steady rise up the corporate ladder (with corresponding increases in income), and a retirement pension.

Today, that "contract" between employer and employee no longer exists in many companies. Why? A confluence of radical changes has rewritten the rules of the workplace. These changes include technological advances, globalization, a boom in entrepreneurship and a proliferation of new, small, fast-moving companies, and a wave of reengineering and restructuring that has led to flatter and leaner organizations.

Such changes mean that the skills required for any company to stay competitive—whether large or small, new or mature—keep shifting at an ever-increasing rate of speed.

Shifting your skills to stay competitive

Today, workers must update and broaden their abilities more frequently and use a wider variety of skills—whether they're employees of a company or entrepreneurs running their own businesses, or whether it's early or late in their professional lives. Middle managers especially have felt the impact of organizational flattening. For instance, managers' responsibilities and roles have shifted so dramatically that many people are no longer sure how to define the term *manager*! And due to layoffs and restructurings in recent decades, many managers have lost their jobs or have had their responsibilities redefined in not-so-desirable ways.

These scenarios can pose difficulties for even the toughest among us. However, there's also a bright side to the picture: As companies reinvent themselves, new opportunities for growth emerge that no one would have dreamed of a few years ago.

You can play a proactive part in these changing times. How? By taking charge of your own career development—that is, by constantly clarifying what you want to do next and learn next and then taking the steps necessary to find those opportunities and obtain that knowledge.

Also, professional development doesn't necessarily mean changing your career or job or discovering your ideal career for the first time, as a person new to the workforce would do. It can also mean growing and increasing your satisfaction *within* your current role and professional path. This is far healthier—and more stimulating—than getting caught in a job rut doing the same thing year after year. And it makes you a far more valuable employee to your company.

Thinking career lattice, not ladder

In today's work world, career development is for *everyone*—no matter what your industry, position, or age. To grasp the differences between today's and yesterday's employment "rules," compare career-ladder thinking with career-lattice thinking, as shown in the table "Examples of career-ladder and career-lattice thinking."

Examples of career-ladder and career-lattice thinking

Career-ladder thinking	Career-lattice thinking
I move up or down the corporate ladder.	I can move up or down *or* side to side.
My boss has all the answers.	My colleagues and I must figure things out.
The longer I stay at the company, the more rewards I'll receive.	The more I improve my learning, contributions, and performance, the more rewards I'll receive.
My company is responsible for its own success.	I and each of my colleagues are responsible for our organization's success.

Thinking strategically about your career

Your company is constantly thinking strategically about its positioning in the industry and the value of its products and services. Likewise, *you* can constantly think strategically about your place in the company and the value of your work interests and skills.

By regularly attending to your development and updating your skills, you become increasingly valuable to your company. You can also derive more and more satisfaction and stimulation from your work.

What if you work for a small company or have launched your own business? You can still think strategically about your career. And you'll probably feel even more responsible for your professional growth. Why? Because, unlike many employees in large corporations, you won't have access to an in-house career center or company-sponsored professional development programs—leaving your career development entirely up to you.

Knowing
Yourself

T HE MOST IMPORTANT step in managing your career is getting to know yourself. This is true whether you're just beginning your career, established in one but wishing you could change in some way, or happy where you are but still wanting to improve certain aspects of it.

Clarifying who you are

Knowing yourself includes articulating things such as what types of work you like to do, what kinds of environments you prefer to work in, what sorts of people you like to work with, what abilities you possess, and what abilities you need to develop. In other words, to define and navigate your career path, you need to identify your most passionate core business interests, your deepest work values, and your strongest skills.

How do you go about identifying these? You have three sources of information: looking inward, asking others, and using formal assessment tools.

Looking inward

To use yourself as an information source, look deep within yourself to identify key themes. You can do this by using checklists or worksheets that help you clarify your core interests, values, and skills. You can also engage in some short mental exercises to get to know yourself better. Here are just a few.

- **Articulate what makes you unique.** Ask yourself what you cherish most about yourself. What is most special about you? What are your unique gifts?

- **Look for imagery.** Leaf through some magazines and find a picture that you think best represents who you are. Ask yourself why you chose that particular image.

- **Envision your entire life.** Imagine that you are at the end of your life, looking back over your entire work history. Finish these sentences: "I am most proud of _____."
  "I wish I had done more of _____."

Notice what the results of these activities suggest about your interests, values, and skills.

Asking others

The people who know you best often become excellent sources of information about your work interests, values, and abilities. Indeed, if you imagine yourself as the CEO of your own professional growth, you can think of these people as your board of directors.

Try these activities to build self-knowledge with the help of your personal board.

- **Consult your colleagues.** If you work in a large or small organization, ask colleagues, "What's my reputation in the company? What am I best known for?"

- **Interview your friends.** Pick five or six people who know you well. Ask them questions such as these: "What four words would you use to describe me?" "If your best friend asked you to tell her more about me, what would you say?" "What do you see as my driving force? What makes me tick?"

- **Ask people who know you well to write letters to you—anonymously (to get their most honest feedback).** Invite several people to write a letter to you, about you. (Tip: Choose a mix of people, for example, a colleague, a supervisor, a family member, a college friend, a social friend, your partner, and even an adult son or daughter.)

Provide your board members with a form that lists the following questions and includes spaces where they can write or type their answers. Ask them to use the third person ("Pat enjoys . . .") in their responses.

- "What would be the ideal work for me?"

- "What seems to make me most fulfilled and excited?"

- "What work should I stay away from, and why?"

- "What about myself do I have trouble seeing?"

- "What aspects of myself do I need to change to be more successful?"

- "What aspects of myself should I not change?"

Collect all the responses and look for common themes. These themes will provide clues to your interests, values, and skills. Be sure to thank your board members for their honesty and thoughtful attention. They'll appreciate knowing that you're using the information and insight they've provided.

Using formal assessment tools

A broad array of formal assessment tools can help you clarify your deepest interests, values, and skills. For some of these, you might want to see a career counselor, who will administer the tests and interpret them for you. For others, you can take the tests and interpret the results yourself. CareerLeader, a career management tool created by the mentors, is an online assessment tool you can use on your own as well as with the help of a career counselor.

Tip: To pick the right career counselor for you, ask potential candidates—whether internal or independent— to describe their philosophy, explain what kinds of clients and questions they typically work with, and describe their successes and the methods they used to achieve them. If you're a successful executive or manager, look for someone with a lot of experience helping people at your level. Be leery of counselors who use the same approach with everyone. This can indicate poor training and limited ability. In career counseling, one size *doesn't* fit all.

If your company's human resources department has a career counselor who uses assessment tools, pay a visit and see if you can schedule a time to take any tests you're interested in. If that option isn't available, consider hiring a career counselor to help you with the tests.

Knowing when it's time for a change

There's another important part of knowing yourself: recognizing when it's time to explore new work opportunities. The signals can differ for each person. The table "Are you ready for a change?" can help you determine whether you've outgrown your current role and would relish new experiences. Check "Yes" or "No" for each statement.

Are you ready for a change?

I am experiencing . . .	Yes	No
A feeling of dread when Monday morning rolls around		
Envy of what others are doing for work		
Restlessness		
Boredom		
A recurring sense of repetition in my work		
A growing interest in nonwork areas of my life, such as a course I'm taking or a home-improvement project I'm considering		
Inability to see a future that I want to move toward		
A tendency to overreact to small problems		
A need for more intellectual challenge, financial compensation, autonomy, or another major work reward value		

Interpreting your score: If you checked "Yes" for most of these statements, you are probably ready for a change in your professional life.

Understanding
Business Interests

Y OUR CORE BUSINESS interests—the activities that you most enjoy doing—are the most important elements to understand about yourself when you're considering reshaping your career. By gaining familiarity the full range of possible core business interests, you can begin determining which ones you might have.

Eight core interests

Through extensive research, we have identified eight core business interests that people can have. Your core interests remain relatively stable over your lifetime, so they're an excellent foundation on which to base your career. We've organized the eight interests into the following three categories. The first category, *Application of Expertise*, includes these interests:

- **Application of Technology:** getting involved in the inner workings of things; being curious about better ways to use technology to solve business problems; feeling comfortable with mathematics, computer programming, and physical models of reality

- **Quantitative Analysis:** engaging in problem solving that relies on mathematical analysis—frequently, but not always, financial analysis

- **Theory Development and Conceptual Thinking:** taking broadly conceptual approaches to problem solving; having interest in and comfort with abstract ideas, imagination, theory, plans, scenarios, and forecasts

- **Creative Production:** taking part in highly creative activities, ones in which you bring something new into being—whether that something is a creative product as such or a new way to make sealing wax

The second category, *Working with People*, consists of the following interests:

- **Counseling and Mentoring:** helping others to grow and developing relationships as an integral part of business work
- **Managing People and Relationships:** dealing with people and interpersonal issues daily

And the third category, *Control and Influence*, is made up of these interests:

- **Enterprise Control:** having ultimate decision-making authority for an enterprise, division, or project: the power to set the strategy and to ensure that the strategy is carried out
- **Influence through Language and Ideas:** persuading others through the skilled use of written and spoken language (whether you're talking to one person, a small group, or a large audience)

Figuring out your core interests

Most people have between one and three core business interests, some of which may be stronger than others. For example, you may be fascinated by quantitative puzzles and feel great satisfaction in helping other people learn to solve problems as well. Your core interests may manifest themselves differently at different times. For example, if your interests are Creative Production and Application of Technology, perhaps in childhood you loved writing stories and plays. Then, in your teenage years, you enjoyed devising mechanical gadgets. Later, as an adult, you desired a career in design engineering or movie production.

You can identify your core business interests by learning what typical activities express the various interests and then seeing which of those activities you find most appealing. The table "A closer look at core business interests" gives examples of such activities.

A closer look at core business interests

CATEGORY 1: APPLICATION OF EXPERTISE

Application of Technology	Quantitative Analysis
Examples:	*Examples:*
• Engineering • Programming computers • Planning production tasks and systems • Designing product and processes • Analyzing processes • Analyzing systems • Crafting and manufacturing • Researching	• Analyzing cash flows and investments • Analyzing market research • Forecasting • Building computer models • Creating production schedules • Performing accounting tasks

Theory Development and Conceptual Thinking	Creative Production
Examples:	*Examples:*
• Developing economic theories • Developing business models	• Designing new products • Marketing and advertising

- Analyzing the competition
- Designing "big-picture" strategies
- Designing processes
- Teaching business theory

- Generating new ideas
- Developing innovative approaches and solutions
- Being an entrepreneur
- Managing projects
- Conducting public relations

CATEGORY 2: WORKING WITH PEOPLE

Counseling and Mentoring

Managing People and Relationships

Examples:

- Coaching, training, teaching
- Performing organizational development
- Managing human resources
- Fostering mentoring-oriented management
- Supporting and developing people
- Providing feedback and advice

Examples:

- Managing others to accomplish the goals of the business
- Directing
- Supervising
- Leading others
- Motivating
- Taking care of day-to-day operations

CATEGORY 3: CONTROL AND INFLUENCE

Enterprise Control

Influence through Language and Ideas

Examples:

- Controlling resources to actualize a business vision
- Setting the strategic direction for a company, business unit, work team, or division
- Having ultimate decision-making authority
- Making deals
- Holding ultimate responsibility for business transactions, such as trades, sales, and so on

Examples:

- Negotiating
- Deal-making
- Conducting public relations
- Selling
- Persuading
- Designing advertising campaigns
- Communicating ideas through writing or speaking

To determine your core interests, you could also try these exercises.

- Think about times when you've been so absorbed in what you were doing that you lost track of time—whether what you were doing was work related or not. (Psychologists call this the experience of *flow*.) Then try to understand what really pulled you into that flow and how that might translate into something you do at work.
- Think about whether you're envious of any particular colleagues. That is, do they have jobs that you wish *you* had? Ask yourself what activities these people perform that you wish you could do. Then, recall previous jobs you've held. Ask yourself what kinds of activities you kept gravitating toward.
- Remember times when you've been working on projects. Which *stages* of a project excite you the most—the planning stage? Implementation? Follow-up?

What do the answers to all these questions suggest about your core business interests?

Finally, consider using assessment tools or other self-reflection exercises and activities that can help you gain insights about yourself.

Clarifying Your Work Reward Values

WHILE IT'S VITAL to understand your core business interests in shaping your career, your work values are also important.

What are work reward values?

People mean many different things when they speak of values. For example, many of us speak of family values, national values, or spiritual values. But *work reward values* constitute a special set of values. Specifically, they're the values you place on the various rewards that you might get in return for performing your job. They refer to the rewards that motivate you to do any parts of your work that you're not intrinsically interested in—the dessert you get for eating the things you may like a little less well.

Here are some examples of work reward values.

- **Financial rewards** include financial security and stability. They might take the form of a predictable salary, specific types of benefits, future employment, and the opportunity to acquire wealth.

- **Task rewards** include intellectual challenge and variety.

- **People rewards** are associated with affiliation—the opportunity to work with colleagues you like and admire. They might also include getting recognition from your superiors.

- **Career rewards** provide you with access to people and opportunities that will position you well for your next career move.

- **Lifestyle rewards** such as work/life balance allow you time to pursue other important aspects of your life, such as family or leisure activities.

Why clarify your work reward values?

Clarifying your values offers several benefits. For one thing, it increases the likelihood that you'll choose satisfying work. It may be difficult to find one position that satisfies all of your desires. But if what you're doing for work doesn't provide *enough* of the rewards that you consider most important, you probably won't remain happy in it for very long.

Moreover, clarifying your values lets you shop more efficiently for the right developmental opportunities. Just as you can evaluate a potential computer purchase much more quickly if you keep a few must-have features in mind, you can judge a work opportunity more wisely if you remember your most crucial rewards.

Finally, clarifying your values helps you match them to the culture of an organization or a department. Work rewards manifest themselves in a workplace's culture—the way people do things, what they expect, what they think is most important, and so forth. A large company's different departments (for example, engineering, sales, or human resources) might have *markedly* different cultures. By knowing your values, you can pick the culture that will provide those rewards.

What Would YOU Do?

Getting to Know Me, Getting to Know All about Me

C ARLY HAS BEEN manager of new business development for ZyMold for five years. One evening after a long day, she got together with Tonya, a friend who had recently changed jobs. Carly found herself feeling envious as Tonya excitedly described her new position. Carly mentioned that she recently received a raise and retention bonus, but she just wasn't as enthusiastic about her work as she once was. She told Tonya that although she likes her team, she senses that something's missing from her work life.

Tonya replied, "It sounds like you need to take a close look at how you feel about your job. Maybe the work just isn't a good fit for you anymore." Carly agreed. But later that night, she found herself wondering exactly what to do next to reshape her career. Should she organize a couple of informational interviews? Talk with someone in HR about job openings elsewhere in the company? Where should she begin?

What would YOU do? See *What You COULD Do*.

Strategies for clarifying your work reward values

Most people are pretty clear on what work rewards motivate them most strongly. But if you need help clarifying your work reward values, one way is to use checklists or worksheets such as the ones provided in the Tips and Tools section of this book.

Another strategy is to analyze experiences you've had in the work world. For example, suppose you've held a position where the rewards you got for the work (perhaps job security or task variety) just didn't matter to you. In this case, ask yourself what would have motivated you more in that role.

Or recall a time when you interviewed for a job, and the interviewer was talking at length about a reward that you just didn't care about. But when he switched gears to a different reward, you found yourself far more interested. This response to discussion of more appealing rewards can clue you in further to your work reward values.

NOTE: In clarifying work reward values, many people face a common temptation to list values they think they *should* have—such as altruism—and to avoid listing values they think they *shouldn't* have—such as desire for prestige or financial gain. Be as honest as you possibly can when articulating your values. Genuine answers will make it much easier for you to evaluate and choose the best possible work opportunities for you.

Steps for Clarifying Your Work Reward Values

1. Write all the work rewards you can think of on index cards, one reward per card.

2. On each card, write a short statement about what that reward means to you. For example, your idea of work/life balance might be working no more than forty hours a week.

3. Scatter the index cards on a table.

4. Arrange the cards in order of importance. If two or more rewards seem equally important to you, place them side by side. If you decide that a reward has no real importance to you after all, set that card aside.

5. Note the order you've settled on. Don't worry about whether you're having trouble deciding which of two seemingly equally important rewards should come first. Just draw a picture that summarizes what you see happening at this stage.

6. Set the stack of cards aside for a week or two.

7. Revisit the exercise to see if anything has shifted.

8. Think of your top three or four rewards as your shopping list when you're considering new developmental opportunities.

What You COULD Do.

Remember Carly's concern about what to do next to begin reshaping her career?

Carly should start by assessing how well her current role fits her core business interests and reward values. She can begin by compiling a record of her thoughts and feelings about her work responsibilities and environment. This record should consist of a private, running list of what she likes and doesn't like about her job or work environment. The entries could be about her own role as well as other people's work and about tasks, relationships, or the work environment itself. Entries might range from simple ("I need to work near a window") to more complex ("I can't stand working alone for long periods of time").

Honesty is key in creating such a record. Carly should see what themes and patterns emerge in the entries. And she needs to consider what these themes tell her about her core business interests and reward values. For example, perhaps the entries in her list suggest that she is most stimulated by helping others or applying technology to business problems. And perhaps they indicate that she feels happiest in a role that offers a collaborative work environment, job security, or intellectual challenge.

(continued)

By gaining insight into her core business interests and reward values, Carly will be well on her way to generating ideas for re-shaping her current role so that it's more satisfying or for moving to a new role at ZyMold or elsewhere.

Assessing Your Skills

I N ADDITION TO clarifying your core business interests and work reward values, it's helpful to assess your skills—the abilities you possess and those you may want to develop in order to excel in a given role. To assess your skills, start by gaining familiarity with the types of skills generally found in the workplace.

Understanding types of skills

As you progress through your work life, you acquire many different skills from a broad range of experiences and training. Skills fall into a number of categories, and there are different ways to describe them. The table "Skill categories" shows some examples.

Skill categories

Category	Examples
Communication	Making presentations, writing marketing copy, interviewing job candidates
Technology	Working with spreadsheets, using graphics or presentation software, designing circuit boards
Finance	Creating a budget, assessing costs, preparing business plans
Supervision	Hiring employees, delegating tasks, assessing people's performance
Management	Managing projects, leading a change initiative, solving business problems

Knowing your strongest skills

As you begin exploring developmental opportunities at your organization, you'll need to know which skills they require. That way, you can decide to what extent these opportunities will allow you to do one or more of the following:

- Use skills you already have in abundance

- Stretch skills that you possess to some degree but would like to strengthen

- Obtain entirely new skills

The first step, though, is to take stock of your existing skills and to assess which ones are your strongest. There are several ways to do this. For example, you can experiment with assessment tools, checklists, and short exercises (like the ones presented in the Tips and Tools section). You can ask your friends, family, and colleagues to give their opinions about what you do best. And you can consult a career counselor.

Articulating your transferable skills

When assessing your skills, it's especially important to identify your transferable skills. These are skills that have value regardless of the business context in which you're using them. Transferable skills include writing, motivating others, organizing data, and interpreting information.

Why is it important to know your transferable skills? Knowing this information allows you to widen the selection of potentially interesting work opportunities to include all those in which you would use your transferable skills. It also helps you avoid the common misconception that, in order to try a new work area, you need to develop a whole new set of skills. You may realize you *don't* necessarily need to go back to school to develop new skills for a different opportunity. When you know your skills, you can market yourself to potential new supervisors in a whole new area of work by pointing out your transferable skills.

TRANSFERABLE SKILLS *n* Abilities that have value regardless of the business context in which they are being used.

Four key points about skills

In assessing your skills, keep these points in mind.

- Skills are a threshold variable in your ability to do a job successfully. You need *enough* of a certain skill (being able to lift 50-pound bags, for example), but in many cases, having a lot more of that same skill (being able to lift *500*-pound bags) won't make you any *more* successful.

- Skills are much less stable than interests or work reward values. That is, you can strengthen existing skills or acquire new ones through practice, training, and new experiences. And you can let skills deteriorate if you no longer use them on a regular basis.

- It's perfectly okay to have both strengths and weaknesses. Often, when people begin exploring new positions at work, they assume that they have to be good at just about everything. The fact is, we all have both strengths and weaknesses—that's part of what makes us who we are. Don't feel bad if you lack certain skills; everyone does.

- You need to weigh the benefits of developing new skills. Investing in skill development can be costly, in terms of time, effort, and money (possibly). So, when you're evaluating a potential new opportunity at work, spend some time deciding whether you want to invest in developing the skills that the opportunity requires.

Steps for Defining and Obtaining New Skills

1. Identify what you need to learn and why you need to learn it. Consider a variety of skill types—including functional, transferable skills (such as clear writing or working with numbers), task-oriented skills (for example, writing a computer program in a particular language or assembling a particular consumer product), personal skills (including being organized or juggling many tasks at once), interpersonal skills (such as the ability to lead a discussion or negotiate), and industry-specific skills (those required for performance of a particular job).

2. Select the ways you might be able to learn. Cast your net wide! You've got many different options for learning at your

disposal—in addition to the more commonly known ones such as going back to school. Also, different people learn best through different learning channels and materials. Then think about which channels and materials work best for you—home-study courses, direct observation of someone else, internships, volunteer work, films, workshops, and online learning programs are all good possibilities.

3. Conduct research to identify specific learning options. Explore resources such as professional associations, career centers, adult-education centers, university extension offices, and the Internet.

4. Analyze your learning options, weighing matters such as quality of instruction, cost, time required, and location.

5. Develop a training strategy and schedule. Clarify how and by when you'll acquire the skills.

Finding Developmental Opportunities at Your Company

O NCE YOU'VE ASSESSED your skills, the next step is to get a complete picture of who you are by combining the skills information with what you learned about your core business interests and work values. You can now use this knowledge and information to redefine your current role. You can also begin evaluating the growth opportunities available at your company and pick the most appropriate ones for you.

Throughout this process of gaining knowledge and information about yourself and your interests, values, and skills, remember: Interests and values matter the most. When evaluating a career development opportunity, make sure that it matches your *core business interests* and *work values*. If it does, you may well decide to obtain the skills that will help you perform in that new position.

Starting the search

You've worked to identify your deepest business interests, clarify your most important work reward values, and assess your strongest skills. Maybe you've even defined a career opportunity target. What's the next step on the path? Many companies have an explicit process in place to enable employees to explore and pursue new opportunities. For example, your organization might suggest that you visit its career management center, review the job bank, and then follow the guidelines.

Other companies ask that you first talk with your supervisor. That way, he or she can become aware of your search and help you either redefine your current role or identify potential opportunities elsewhere in the organization.

Indeed, in most organizations, helping direct reports clarify their goals and find appropriate growth opportunities are important responsibilities for managers. By supporting you in this way, your manager helps the organization retain a valued employee—a key step for any company that wants to stay competitive in today's economy. You can provide the same kind of support for your direct reports.

There are many ways to identify potential growth opportunities throughout your company. The key is to make sure you *know your company*.

- In simplest terms, what work does the organization do?

- What are your company's biggest needs and challenges?

- How do you think you could contribute to your company's efforts in ways that suit your deepest interests, values, and skills?

Finding out what people do

You also need to find out what kinds of work people do throughout the organization. Knowing this will give you a big picture of how the company functions. Of course, gathering all this information takes some research and a willingness to get to know people who can help you. Here are some ideas to get you started.

First, *use your company's career management resources.* Many companies offer numerous ways to learn about growth opportunities. Find out what they are—and take advantage of them. These include:

- Career centers staffed by career counselors and research specialists

- Internal networks of people who are willing to talk with any fellow employee about their jobs

- Opportunities to sample different jobs by filling in for colleagues who are on sabbatical

- Job banks describing all the positions available in the organization

- Reference materials and training to help you create a professional growth plan and hone your résumé-writing and interviewing skills

- In-house courses on various subjects and skills related to jobs within the company

- Tuition reimbursement programs for college or vocational school

Second, *build your network.* Networking simply means getting to know people in your organization who can help you learn about and pursue career opportunities. To become an expert networker, ask yourself: "Who knows the most about what's going on in the organization?" Then seek out opportunities to meet those people and talk with them about your search.

> **Tip:** In your company directory, identify people
> who do work that interests you, and get to know them.
> Tell them you're clarifying your professional development
> goals, and ask to have a conversation with them
> sometime about their work.

Third, *cultivate relationships with mentors*—experts from whom you can learn, in detail, about specific kinds of work and strategies for defining a career path. Mentors can be people who work in your organization or outside your organization, members of professional associations—anyone whose experience and knowledge you respect.

> **Tip:** Establish mentoring relationships with
> (1) one person within your company (your company
> mentor), (2) another person who has mastered the area
> of expertise you're interested in (your skill mentor), and
> (3) someone whose overall career path you find enviable
> (your career strategy mentor). If possible, at least one
> mentor should be someone outside your company.

And fourth, *consult a career counselor*. Many organizations have career counselors on staff who can advise you on how to spot potential development opportunities. If your organization provides this service, make an appointment. If not, consider having a couple of sessions with an independent career counselor. These professionals' services can be pricey, so be sure to shop around for the best choice for you. On the other hand, someone who charges more but can help you better and faster may ultimately be a bargain for you.

Choosing the right growth opportunities

When making decisions about which growth opportunities to pursue, ask yourself questions such as these: "How good is the fit between the position and my interests, values, and skills?" "How good is the fit between the position and who I want to become?" (That is, "What kinds of *learning opportunities* does this position offer me?") The best developmental assignments are ones in which the fit is imperfect—the position will stretch you by offering challenges that encourage you to learn new skills and acquire new knowledge.

Of course, stretch positions carry some risk. You won't be able to make your most productive contribution right away. After all, you'll need time to learn the new dimensions of the job. The challenge is to pick an opportunity that doesn't stretch you *too* much or carry *too* great a risk. As a general rule of thumb, the risk is probably too great if it seems that you'll need more than six months to learn enough to make a meaningful contribution.

Getting the skills you need

There are lots of ways to enhance your skills, including on-site training, adult-education courses, distance learning, and online courses. One key thing to remember, though, is that you *don't* always need to go back to school to make a major change in your career. Before you commit to spending a lot of money (and time) on a new degree, do some research to make sure there isn't a more affordable and less time-consuming way to master the skills that your new position requires.

Getting the information you need

Once you've identified possible development opportunities, it's time to arrange some informational interviews. You can conduct

Steps for Preparing for an Informational Interview

1. Think of three to five individuals who are currently doing the kind of work you're interested in.
2. Contact them (by phone, by e-mail, or in person).
3. Set a time and meeting place for an appointment.
4. Prepare a list of questions you'd like to ask the interviewee.

these interviews with people who are currently doing the kind of work you're interested in, with supervisors, or with department or division heads who can give you valuable information about the work.

Informational interviewing is less formal than actual job interviewing because it gives you a chance to learn more about positions of interest and helps you get to know potential new supervisors and other people in departments or divisions of interest. It also lets you showcase your talents and may give you further insight into additional interesting positions. (Even if an interview reveals that a particular new job wouldn't work out for you, you can use the encounter as another networking opportunity by asking the interviewee to suggest more people for you to talk with.)

The key to setting up informational interviews is to be sincere and honest when contacting potential interviewees. If you're nervous about contacting people, remember that you're asking for information, not a job offer. Also, most people are happy to talk about their work, if you respect their time (ask for no more than twenty minutes) and clearly value the information they offer. Finally, people are especially open to meeting with you if you've been referred to them by someone they know and respect. So, broach the subject of an interview by saying something like, "Hello, my name is _____. I'm currently working as a _____ and am interested in learning about _____. My colleague _____ mentioned that you'd be a great person for me to talk with. Could I have twenty minutes of your time when it's most convenient for you?"

Steps for Defining Your Career Target

1. Review what you've discovered about your core business interests, your work reward values, and your skills.
2. List and describe the career opportunities at your organization.
3. Draw three concentric circles. That is, draw a large circle on a piece of paper. Within that large circle, draw a somewhat smaller circle. (Make the second circle small enough so that you have room to write between the two circles.) Within that somewhat smaller circle, draw another circle. That central, smallest circle is your career bull's-eye.
4. Identify the opportunities that match your core business interests. In the outermost circle of your career bull's-eye, write down these opportunities. This is your core interests circle.
5. In your core interests circle, underline or highlight those opportunities that also match your most important work reward values.
6. Copy the opportunities you underlined in step 5 into the next inner circle. This is your important values circle.

7. Now underline or highlight those opportunities in your important values circle that also match the skills you now possess or skills you could obtain relatively easily.

8. Copy the opportunities you underlined in step 7 into the centermost circle—your bull's-eye. You've now defined your career target: work that matches your core business interests, your most important work reward values, and your skills.

Steps for Sculpting Your Job

1. Look at the career bull's-eye you created in Steps for Defining Your Career Target.

2. Ask yourself, "Where is the mismatch between my job and the kinds of opportunities that are in my career target?"

3. Divide a piece of paper into three columns. Write "Interests" at the top of the left-hand column, "Values" at the top of the middle column, and "Skills" at the top of the right-hand column. Write down every area you can think of in which your current role does not suit your core business interests, work reward values, and/or skills.

4. Try to think of ways to reshape your current role so that it more closely matches your core interests, values, and skills.

5. Talk with your supervisor about redefining your current role so as to get a better match. When you meet with your supervisor, start by stating the reason you want to brainstorm ways to sculpt your job: "My current role doesn't suit me as well as it

could because _____." (Remember to use the language of core interests, values, and skills.) If possible, be ready to offer solutions and ideas for reshaping your current role so that it's a better match for you and your organization. (Don't just bring a problem; bring a problem and a solution.) Your solutions should include explanations of who will handle any responsibilities you want to let go.

Helping Others Manage Their Careers

E VERY TIME SOMEONE helps someone else—through networking, informational interviewing, and so forth—that person becomes willing to help others in turn. So by helping others, you become part of a constant, informal networking process—a web of people who are willing to provide and receive help.

For example, imagine that one day, Victor, who works in a different department than yours, asks if you know any good engineers he could talk to about making some changes in his career. You do, and you give him a few names. Months later, you might run across Victor and realize that he could help you by recommending, say, some marketing specialists you could talk to about the nature of their work.

Putting your organization first

Just as your colleagues can help you clarify your professional goals and identify growth opportunities in your company, you can do the same for your direct reports or colleagues. In fact, by supporting them in this way, you're doing what's best for your organization.

When you help your direct reports find stimulation and satisfaction in their work, you put your organization first in two ways. First, you encourage talented, ambitious people to stay with the company, so the organization retains valuable employees. You thus support your firm in its efforts to build a stronger workforce. Second, you also help the organization cut costs. After all, finding, hiring, and training replacements are all expensive activities.

Tip: Don't be uncomfortable if a direct report tells you that he or she would like to make some work changes. It doesn't necessarily mean that the person no longer wants to report to you or is deeply unhappy at work, or that he or she is thinking about leaving the company. All it means is that the person is wisely taking charge of his or her career development path.

Speaking the language of interests, values, and skills

To support your direct reports' professional goals, you have to become aware of those goals. An excellent way to become—and stay—aware is to have regular professional development reviews (PDRs) with each of your direct reports.

Try making PDRs part of performance reviews, or conduct them separately. Whichever way you decide to schedule PDRs, make sure you frame the discussion in terms of *core business interests, work reward values,* and *skills.* This focuses the meeting and helps you both talk in specific terms about the person's goals.

Fostering a career management mindset

You can help direct reports adopt a career management mindset and search for opportunities in several ways.

- **Redefine a current role:** Consider redefining a current role so that it better matches the person's interests, values, and skills.

- **Help them network:** Identify individuals in the company who you think could provide growth opportunities, guidance, insight, and even more networking opportunities for your employees. Offer strategies for meeting those individuals, or help to arrange meetings.

- **Evaluate options:** Once you and a direct report have identified possible opportunities, help the person evaluate these opportunities' fit and learning potential. Again, use the language of interests, values, and skills in discussing an opportunity's potential.

Do you supervise managers who have direct reports? If so, you can further reinforce the message that helping others manage their professional development is something your company values. How? Reward managers who excel at this responsibility. Consider evaluating your managers' success in this area as a regular part of performance reviews. And if possible at your organization, tie their compensation to their performance in developing their own direct reports' careers.

Managing Stress

Overload
and Toxic Worry

The word on worry

Are worry and stress really such bad things? Or are we just making a big deal out of a normal state of mind and feeling? Some worry or stress is a necessary and important part of our lives, but in today's fast-paced work world, these natural human responses often spiral out of control and become toxic to our productivity, our peace of mind, and our health. Just see what some experts have to say:

"According to a University of Chicago survey, more than 40% of Americans suffer stress in the workplace."

—NPR, *Morning Edition*

"Job stress today accounts for more than 50% of the 550 million workdays lost annually because of absenteeism."

—K. R. S. Edstrom

"Information anxiety is a chronic malaise, a pervasive fear that we're about to be overwhelmed by the very material we need to master in order to function in this world."

—Richard Saul Wurman

"Job stress [is] a world-wide epidemic."

—World Health Organization

Why be concerned about stress?

So, why be concerned about stress, particularly in the workplace? There are many reasons. What seems normal and familiar—a feeling of worry and anxiety about your daily activities—may be preventing you or your team members from reaching personal and professional goals. Left unchecked, toxic stress can:

- **Reduce productivity.** Toxic stress contributes to decreased productivity, absenteeism, and employee turnover. When employees start making mistakes or slowing down on the job, stay home to avoid stressful work situations, or even quit, hoping to find a less stressful position somewhere else, the productivity of your team or the people you supervise can be directly affected.

- **Affect health.** Too much prolonged stress can make you physically ill and can even kill you. Your body reacts to stress as it would to any dangerous physical situation, raising blood pressure and alerting the senses. This response protects you and can be beneficial for a brief time; however, prolonged stress, worry, and anxiety can strain your body beyond its limits.

- **Drain energy.** Excess worry, stress, and anxiety can drain you of energy, causing your work and your personal life to suffer. You need energy to concentrate well, respond effectively, and judge situations appropriately. Worry uses up your energy, depriving you of the physical, mental, or emotional resources needed to do the job well.

- **Damage relationships.** Stress can disrupt relationships—whether at work or at home. While mismatched personalities in work situations can cause interpersonal conflicts,

What WOULD You Do?

What—Me Worry?

WHEN DANIEL ACCEPTED the promotion, he felt confident that he would be able to handle the increased responsibilities that came with the new position. One month into the job, however, Daniel wondered if he had made the wrong decision. Managing ten direct reports was a full-time job in itself. In addition, he was responsible for generating a new marketing plan, overseeing a huge budget, and serving on multiple task forces. Even though Daniel was staying on top of things, he felt increasingly overwhelmed and tired. He hadn't eaten a proper meal in days. Leaving the office at 8:00 p.m. had become the norm. He wished there was something he could do to make things better, but what?

stress can accentuate these negative feelings or aggravate existing situations, causing small problems to seem large and disturbing the functioning of an entire team.

"More heart attacks occur on Mondays between 6:00 a.m. and noon than during any other time."
—Dr. Harry Dassah

The basic equation of worry

What causes toxic worry? When you feel vulnerable to the perceived threats in your world *and* you feel that you have less power to control your world, your level of worry and anxiety will often increase. In mathematical terms:

Increased vulnerability + decreased power = increased worry

A sense of *increased vulnerability* causes you to exaggerate danger, so that a small problem becomes a huge nightmare. For example, if one month your department's direct costs exceed its budget, you might imagine that the entire year's budget will be engulfed by unforeseen costs. A feeling of *decreased power* causes you to underestimate or forget the power you have to combat danger. For instance, when confronted with the cost overrun, you might forget that you have the power to assess the causes of the overrun and make adjustments to remedy the situation in the following months. *Increased worry* hinders you from making rational decisions and taking positive actions to resolve problems.

This basic equation of worry expresses how toxic worry can arise not from actual danger but from imagined peril. It helps explain how a worried mind can be very creative in anticipating threatening situations that are unlikely to occur.

Bad things really do happen

It is true, however, that bad things really do happen, and at times what seems to be excessive worry is actually appropriate for the situation. To illustrate, if your company is unexpectedly acquired by another, fears of downsizing may be perfectly justified. Or if you're an entrepreneur facing a cash-flow squeeze, and you know the bank could suddenly call in your line of credit, you may feel justified in fearing such an event.

In these situations, the "work of worry," or good worry, can give you the energy you need to deal with the problems. By anticipating the reality, you can prepare possible solutions. The important thing is to know the difference between healthy, protective worry that can help you—and toxic worry that can harm you.

What You COULD Do.

Remember Daniel's worries about the pressures of his new job?

Daniel could follow a rational, step-by-step process to examine and improve his stress level. The Evaluate-Plan-Remediate approach works by breaking down the problems that are causing stress into smaller, more manageable units that can be resolved. First, Daniel should identify the problem at hand—namely, that he's overworked and has too many responsibilities. Next, he should think about structuring his time differently. He should set reasonable goals, prioritize them, and break them down into manageable tasks. After that, he should take direct action. He should meet with his supervisor and discuss ways to relieve his workload or delegate some of his responsibilities. By confronting and taking charge of his situation, Daniel will likely reduce his stress level.

Positive Stress and Productive Worry

The dynamic power of worry

Because bad things do happen and because there are high-tension times when we have to be alert, we do need some worry to survive. Worry is our natural defense to a threatening situation, helping us to react quickly and effectively. So up to a point, worry and anxiety are healthy responses.

At first, as anxiety or worry increases, performance also increases. But at a certain point, anxiety becomes excessive and begins to depress performance. An important goal of every businessperson is to find that level of anxiety that will bring about peak performance while avoiding the additional anxiety that becomes toxic to your team or direct reports, as well as to your professional and personal health.

The business value of wise worry

When worry moves from personal fear to clear-headed anticipation, worry energy can make you productive and creative, helping you to discover new solutions to business challenges. Some high-tension worry at work can give you the impetus and adrenaline needed to focus more clearly and perform at a higher level. For example, healthy, positive stress can energize you for action when you have to:

- Meet critical deadlines

- Present an exciting proposal

- Solve new problems

- Feel in control

- Contribute to a team effort

- Learn new skills

- Start a new job

- Deal with a crisis

"Good worry is informed anticipation."
  —Edward M. Hallowell, MD

Wise worry in anticipation can help you prepare for these events, and positive stress during an event can give you the power and vigor to get the job done.

Different strokes for different folks

Some people actually thrive in the high-risk world of trading in the futures market or investing in high-tech start-ups or meeting creative goals in advertising. But other folks prefer a more stable work environment, something more predictable and manageable. The downside of stress is that too much can lead to early burnout and too little can make it easy for people to underproduce. But for each person there is a level of stress that helps that person maximize his or her work goals.

Assessing Your Stress Level

Do you have a problem?

Wise worry helps many businesspeople perform effectively by giving them the foresight and insight to solve business problems. But toxic worry can distort their perceptions of problems and hamper their efforts to deal with them.

How, then, can you tell whether the stress you feel is healthy or not? How can you discover if you are a problem worrier at work? Simply put, when worry or stress interferes with your productive work, then you do have a problem. Problem worriers exaggerate fears, spend too much time on nonconstructive concerns, fail to make decisions, and are slow to produce results.

If you suspect, or already know, that stress is a problem for you, your team, or your direct reports, start to assess the severity of the problem by looking at both the work environment and individual responses to that environment.

Major work stressors

The common causes of stress in the workplace are (1) *changes in the workplace*—precipitating events that set off a cycle of negative stress; (2) *an unhealthy work environment*—ongoing, underlying, and systemic problems in the office; or (3) *individual responses*—anxious reactions to normal or abnormal situations in the workplace. Typically, the negative stress and toxic worry a person experiences can be related to more than one stressor. Let's take a closer look at each of these causes of workplace stress.

Stressful changes in the workplace include:

- **Change in workload.** If a company reduces the size of its workforce but not its production levels, employees may be asked to take on additional tasks and increase productivity to make up for the loss of personnel. Or employees may be asked to shoulder additional responsibilities on top of their regular tasks during a period of company expansion. In either case, the extra work may cause both resentment and anxiety.

- **Change in pay.** If an employee receives a reduction in pay (perhaps through a reduction in benefits), this would very likely cause worry about budgeting. But even an increase in pay can cause concern if it puts workers into an increased tax bracket or if they feel that they must perform at a higher level to "earn" the increase.

- **Change of job, assignment, or team.** A new job situation is always a stressful time. Not only does a worker have to learn new skills and processes, but new office or team relationships have to be developed as well. All this takes extra energy and attention that can become toxic stress, preventing workers from doing their best.

- **Change in job security.** In this age of high-tech revolution, large corporation downsizing (which often hits middle management the hardest), expected rapid turnover, and rapidly growing global markets, the threat of losing one's job seems to be more constant.

Work environments can feel particularly stressful if employees must contend with:

- **Work overload.** When companies downsize or have trouble finding skilled workers, supervisors often expect their current employees to pitch in and make up the difference in time and labor. Work overload is often the result, adding stress and strain to an already overextended team.

- **Workaholic office culture.** At some high-pressure organizations, the culture demands that employees work long hours and weekends, whether or not the need is real. This culture is marked by intense competition and exhausted workers.

- **Difficult supervisors.** There are managers whose leadership styles simply don't match the professional needs of their direct reports. Some supervisors, for example, believe that pushing their team will increase productivity when the opposite is often the reality—creating a general sense of fear and worry that undermines productivity. Conflict with a difficult supervisor is a major cause of corporate turnover.

- **Negative coworkers.** If an office is filled with an atmosphere of distrust and dissension, the level of stress rises for everyone involved. The causes may be varied—a personality clash, disproportionate workloads, inappropriate or discourteous behavior—but the negative effect is the same.

Some workplaces can foster anxiety and other negative individual responses. For example:

- **Fear of failure.** If a work environment is one of competition and criticism rather than team building and reinforcement, negative thinking can result, turning external critical messages into internal self-doubt and an increased fear of failure.

- **Low self-esteem.** Closely related to fear of failure, low self-esteem occurs when negative thinking gains control and blocks out or distorts any positive messages. A can't-do attitude is the result.

- **Lack of trust.** A sense of cynicism can pervade a work environment if management claims one set of positive values, such as loyalty and dedication, but then acts in a way that contradicts those values, such as by retooling or downsizing.

- **Loss of collegial community.** Many people feel disconnected at work, left out, forgotten in their cubicles. This sense of isolation is a real problem for self-employed workers, but it's also a growing concern for companies that are connected through computer networks rather than community gathering spaces.

- **Job burnout.** Job burnout is a unique type of stress. It's a serious consequence of the combination of a workaholic culture and toxic stress. You may feel burned out when you feel trapped in your job, unable to see a future in it. You can't manage to handle routine tasks; you're tired, tense, and irritable; and frankly, you just don't care!

Signs of dis-stress

Some of the signs of *dis-stress*, that is, stress gone too far, are easily recognized, but many are not. If you can develop an awareness of these signs, you can judge whether you are a normal worrier or a problem worrier. Stress can affect you and your body in four areas: physical, emotional, behavioral, and mental. "Your dis-stress checklist" can help you determine whether you're suffering manifestations of dis-stress.

Levels of stress

Levels of stress can range from healthy responses in dangerous situations all the way to exaggerated and dysfunctional worry about every aspect of life. Consider your particular situation: Does the level of stress in your workplace promote energy and excitement? Are major work stressors affecting your performance or the work of those around you? Do you or your team members or direct reports show signs of toxic stress?

If stress is a problem for you or for others in your work environment, it's time to face it and deal with it. There are many ways

Your dis-stress checklist

Are you experiencing . . .	Yes	No
Pounding heart		
Elevated blood pressure		
Sweating		
Headache		
Sleep disturbances		
Skin rashes		
Trembling or tics		
Irritability and impatience		
Depression		
Fearfulness		
Low self-esteem		
Envy		
Loss of interest in your job		
Eating too much or too little		
Drinking more alcohol		
Pacing or restlessness		
Increased smoking		
Teeth grinding, nail biting, or other nervous behaviors		
Aggressive driving		
Forgetfulness		
Mind racing or going blank		
Indecisiveness		
Resistance to change		
Diminished sense of humor		
Declining productivity		

Interpreting your responses: If you answered "Yes" to more than half of these statements, you may be suffering from physical, emotional, behavioral, and mental manifestations of dis-stress.

to improve an unhealthy, stress-laden situation. The strategies for dealing with toxic stress in this guide can help most people achieve a healthier stress-performance balance. However, if you or your coworkers or direct reports get stuck, it is important to recognize the extent of the problem and get further professional help.

Taking Charge of Stress

Acceptance—or action?

There are always parts of your life that you cannot change—who you are, where you are, and where you've been. For those facts that simply *are*, acceptance is the healthiest path to take. But for those parts of your life that you *can* change, taking charge by giving yourself the power to change is an exciting prospect. If your stress level is too high, if you worry obsessively, if you are anxious about every little thing, take a deep breath and then take charge. The following sections present basic strategies for taking charge.

Tip: Help your team or direct reports accept the unchangeable elements of the business environment and take charge of what can be changed or reformed.

Reversing the basic equation of worry

The basic equation of worry describes a negative process of increasing worry.

Increased vulnerability + decreased power = increased worry

Taking charge describes the process of reversing this basic equation: Ease worry by reducing your feeling of vulnerability and bolstering your feeling of power.

Decreased vulnerability + increased power = decreased worry

By beginning to take charge, you can decrease your sense of help-lessness, increase your power to perceive the problem more clearly and to discover positive actions you need to take to improve the situation or solve the problem, and quickly diminish the worry that was interfering with your ability to function effectively.

"If worrying can persecute us, it can also work for us, as self-preparation. No stage fright, no performance."
—Adam Phillips

Applying the four-step approach

One way to break out of the negative stress cycle is to take this four-step approach, which gives you a structure for dealing with stress as it occurs.

- **Step 1: stop.** As soon as you begin to feel stress coming on, say, "Stop!" to yourself. For example, your computer freezes just as you're trying to finish your presentation, and you feel that rush of anxiety with failure messages flooding into your mind: "The presentation will fail; I'll fail; I'll be fired." Block those messages before they can be heard by saying, "Stop!" Repeat the message two more times: "Stop! Stop!"

- **Step 2: breathe.** The next step is to breathe. Take a deep breath, filling your diaphragm with air. Hold that breath for eight seconds, and then slowly let the air out. Just as the word "stop" blocks the negative thoughts from your mind, breathing overcomes the tendency to hold your breath when under stress. Focusing on breathing helps you to focus on your stress in a different way.

- **Step 3: reflect.** By interrupting the pattern of stress and giving yourself energy through breathing, you can now focus on the real problem, the cause of the stress. By reflecting on your stress response, you can begin to distinguish the different levels of thought and to sort out rational from irrational stress responses. You can see the practical situation more calmly and realistically and distinguish it from the distortions of your anxiety-influenced thoughts.

- **Step 4: choose.** Finally, with your attention now on the practical problem itself, you can choose to find real solutions. For example, after rebooting your computer you may discover that very little material was lost, or that even without the lost material, you'll still be able to get the information across to your audience using the old-fashioned method of talking it through. What might have seemed a disaster becomes a manageable problem that you were given the power to solve by identifying your options.

Maintaining your work/life balance

Stress occurs in most working situations, but the often conflicting demands of work and personal life can be a major source of stress, worry, and anxiety, both at work and at home. Finding a healthy balance between the two can reduce toxic stress and increase productive energy in all aspects of your life. Keep in mind the following:

- Work and personal life need to be complementary, not conflicting.

- Business priorities need to be identified and then balanced with personal concerns.

- "Whole people" are those whose skills and knowledge overlap in work and in life beyond work.

- Flexible and creative approaches to this balance enhance an employee's performance and energy for both work and personal life.

Steps for Breaking Out of the Negative Stress Cycle

1. Stop the negative messages flooding your mind.
2. Breathe by taking a deep breath and slowly letting the air out.
3. Reflect on the situation.
4. Choose to find a solution.

Turning Worry into Action

A three-step strategy

You already have the means to change the pattern of escalating worry by using the power of your mind. The systematic *Evaluate-Plan-Remediate* approach allows you to examine the process of worry and break it down into smaller, more manageable problem units that can be solved or resolved.

For example, suppose you receive a team e-mail from your supervisor about the agenda for an upcoming budget review meeting. In the past, you've always been asked to present the target revenues for your department, but you have yet to be asked this year. You feel a twist in your stomach, a sign that worry is creeping in. Your thoughts begin to speed up: "Why haven't I been asked? Did someone else get the assignment? Did I do a poor job last time? I must be an idiot! Am I being demoted or eased out?" Using the Evaluate-Plan-Remediate worry-intervention method, you can stop the worry as soon as you start to feel it taking over.

1. **Evaluate:** "Yes, I haven't yet been asked to present the projected revenues at the budget review meeting. That's all I know right now."

2. **Plan:** "I need to get information. I should contact my supervisor and ask her directly if she expects me to present this part of the budget."

3. **Remediate:** "I'll call my supervisor and make an appointment to see her in person."

This simple sequence can replace that sense of panic with an immediate evaluation of the situation and a plan for necessary action. If you can make this process a habit every time you feel that twist in your stomach or twinge in your head, you'll turn your worry into action.

Step 1: evaluate

The key to evaluating the cause of the worry is to confront it. Don't ignore those little signals your body is giving you. They won't go away until you face what causes them. Use the following guidelines for this step.

Name the problem Just giving a name to a problem can help reduce stress because by identifying the specific problem, you've already eliminated all other possibilities. Naming makes things more manageable. Discover the stress-creating pattern that describes your situation. For example, do you take on too many responsibilities? Find it difficult to balance work and life issues? Work in the wrong job? Have problems with colleagues or supervisors? Procrastinate when a deadline looms?

Think constructively about the problem This may seem like a difficult step, but all it takes is an honest examination of your own automatic worry process. It requires that you step back and watch yourself in order to identify how your mind leaps from the bad news or perceived danger that triggers the worry to the "awfulizing" of the initial event. Apply these practices:

- **Examine your automatic thoughts.** Monitor your automatic thoughts. What words pop into your mind? Write down the words and look at them more objectively. Often you can see how exaggerated they are. For example, do you use negative descriptors (*idiot*, *stupid*) against yourself?

- **Correct errors in logic.** Next, examine your automatic thoughts for errors in logic. For example, why would your supervisor include you in the e-mail message about the budget meeting unless you had a role in that meeting? Your hasty assumption that you were being excluded is an error in logic.

- **Develop alternative hypotheses.** Even though you may leap to the worst-case scenario, there may be other hypotheses that could explain the situation. Your supervisor may have assumed that you were working on the revenue report, or she may have a different task in mind for you.

- **Revise your fundamental assumptions about yourself and your work.** Instead of calling yourself stupid and assuming that the disaster will certainly occur, start becoming your own best supporter. This may prove to be a difficult step to take because these fundamental assumptions can reflect ancient and deep-seated ways of looking at yourself and your world. However, if these assumptions are untrue and block constructive thoughts, they need to be replaced with healthier and more honest ones. The important thing is to discard the distortions that prevent you from achieving rational and productive solutions.

Never worry alone Invite a friend to help as a listening partner. Sharing your worries with the right person can make you feel better by unloading the weight of worry. Just talking out loud about your concerns helps to sort them out and to clarify where your concerns may be valid and where you may be distorting the problem. The listener, at this point, needs simply to listen, rather than trying to solve your problems. Your goal here is to understand your own worry process and gain the power to find your own solutions.

Step 2: plan

Planning ahead can take time and may seem to be a burden, but the value of planning is a more than adequate return on your time investment. Planning can intercept the toxic worry and replace it with effective action. Here are some practices you can apply in advance.

Get the facts Wise worry confronts real problems. Toxic worry exaggerates and misrepresents reality. Brooding about the "what-if" possibilities passively burns up your energy. So get active! Find out what the truth of the matter is. Go to the sources of information, and don't rely on hearsay, gossip, or your own vivid imagination.

Tip: Get help from the right sources—people who have the information you need. Often you don't have the information or tools necessary to attack a problem. Instead of worrying, take control by getting the help you need. Find out who the authority is and where you should look for answers.

Structure your life Much worry results from unstructured living and thinking habits. A cluttered desk with files scattered about means wasted time finding the material you need and the risk of losing important information. In the same way, a mind cluttered with "what-if" possibilities can hide the "that-is" reality. Worried people typically spend more time and energy worrying than they do accomplishing productive tasks.

Structuring your life is being kind and considerate to yourself—organizing your desk helps *you* find things. Structuring your life reduces your risk of losing vital files, information, keys—and also prevents you from losing perspective. Use structure as an anti-anxiety agent: lists, reminders, schedules, rules, and budgets are all methods of structuring your life for your own benefit.

Take the time to structure your space. For example, organize your desk. Use colored file folders with clear labels. Put your keys in the same spot every day. And organize your computer desktop and mailbox. Also structure your *time*:

- Set goals. Decide what you want or need to accomplish in the coming week.

- Prioritize your goals. Break them down into small, manageable activities.

- Use a date book to avoid missing appointments and to stay on target.

- Be fair to yourself: make your plan for the week reasonable.

- Match important activities to the times of your high-energy peaks—the times of the day when you feel most alert and vigorous.

- Save the simple, repetitive tasks for your low-energy periods.

- Avoid getting involved in activities that don't match your goals.

- Be sure to take breaks to restore energy—stand up and stretch, take a short walk, or chat briefly with a colleague.

Tip: If you find the idea of organizing a cause for new worry, ask a friend or colleague—someone whose desk is neat and who is never late to a meeting—to give you a hand. Ask for help from more than one person; you may discover ideas and ways to structure your life that are actually easy and fun!

Step 3: remediate

The next step is to find a remedy for toxic worry. Reason, planning, and action are powerful antidotes to the paralysis of stress and worry. Consider these guidelines.

Take direct action If you've evaluated the problem and planned what you can do about it, then go ahead, take the plunge and just do it! Make the phone call, change your behavior, clean up that desk, connect with a friend, or confront that difficult colleague. Taking action is empowering. Your feeling of vulnerability and your toxic worry will fade.

Let it go Why let go? No matter how much you may want to effect a change, some problems can't be solved by any action on your part. You just have to wait and see how things turn out. Worrying about the matter won't help. For example, if your supervisor suddenly announces a major reorganization, you can't do anything about it until the event happens and you have more information about how it will affect you. You just have to sit tight and wait. Or perhaps you're up for a big promotion, but you won't find out about the decision for a month. You will be better off in every way—physically, emotionally, and mentally—if you can let the worry go until later.

What does letting go mean? Letting go means giving up your sense of control, and this can be difficult to do. Often people feel that if they worry enough, they might affect the outcome. But in those cases and times when control doesn't help and worry only hurts, it's worth the effort to give up both worry and control.

How can you let worry go? Different people have different ways. Some find that meditation helps. Some listen to music or sing a song. Try putting your worry in the palm of your hand and blowing it away. Close your eyes and imagine the worry putting on its coat and hat and walking slowly out of the room. The important thing for you is to say goodbye to useless worry.

Tip: If there's nothing you can do about a problem (or nothing more, if you already worked on it)—if it's simply out of your control—you have to let the worry go. Blow it away, and start a new project, read a different book, walk another path.

Connecting
with Others

Making connections

The Evaluate-Plan-Remediate approach uses reason, logic, and action to confront the exaggerations of toxic worry by increasing the worrier's sense of power and control. Connectedness uses the human need to connect and share with others to reduce the sense of vulnerability. Thus, both approaches help to reverse the basic equation of worry.

In the workplace, connectedness can be feeling that you are part of a company, part of a department, part of a team, working together. Connectedness can also be sharing with friends, with partners, in activities you love.

CONNECTEDNESS *n* **1:** a feeling that you are part of something larger than yourself

Understanding the disconnected workplace

As so many of us sit in our cubicles today, separated from our coworkers and yet not quite alone, we can feel disconnected from the people surrounding us. Entrepreneurs or home-office workers can feel even more isolated. We communicate via e-mails, voice mail, and faxes, rarely speaking one-on-one to a human voice on the telephone, much less face-to-face. With the ability to access large amounts of information on the Internet, we don't even need to speak to a librarian to get the data or knowledge we need to complete a project.

That sense of disconnectedness can aggravate our anxieties, contribute to worry, and increase stress. We can have a difficult time finding someone to talk to, someone with whom we can test our concerns in reality checks; share news, ideas, and resources; or just banter about the latest sports, politics, or company events. The obstacles to connecting that some companies create can seem daunting:

- Treating employees as robots

- Using technical communication instead of human interaction

- Encouraging a competitive desire to hoard information instead of sharing

- Separating employees physically into work cubes

- Overloading employees with extra work

Time, pressure, and competition keep employees hunched over their desks, increasing their stress and ultimately decreasing their productivity.

"Worry gives a small thing a big shadow."
　—Swedish proverb

What WOULD You Do?

Rabbit, Run

ONE MORNING, ELLEN, a manager in the customer service department, overhears a colleague talking about presenting reports at an upcoming meeting. These are reports that *Ellen* usually presents. She wonders whether she did a poor job presenting the reports last time and worries that her supervisor has asked someone else to present them this time because he wasn't satisfied with Ellen's presentation. Ellen realizes that she often feels this way—vulnerable to criticism from supervisors and peers—and she knows that this sense of vulnerability is adding to the stress she is experiencing. Whenever she finds herself wondering if she's going to be criticized, she feels like a frightened rabbit menaced by a predator. And her nervous habits, such as chewing her nails and pulling at her hair, intensify. Ellen knows she needs to address her tendency to feel vulnerable. But she's not sure precisely how to tackle the problem.

Unleashing the power of connectedness

While isolation permits toxic worry to escalate, human contact can deflate toxic worry. The human moment—when two people are face-to-face and listening to each other—gives the worrier a chance to unburden himself or herself of those anxieties, a chance to get a reality check from the listener, a chance to be reassured that he or she is not alone facing apparently overwhelming problems.

The human moment, that one-on-one connection between two people, is essential for combating negative stress and distorted worries, but other forms of positive connectedness are also important and powerful antidotes to stress and worry. Everyone in the workplace—individual employees, supervisors, and self-employed workers—needs to strive to increase their own and others' connections to people they trust and to ideas and things they care about.

Using connections to foster community

Two kinds of connectedness are vital in the workplace: connectedness to colleagues and connectedness to a mission.

Connectedness to colleagues This takes effort on your part, but it's worth it. Seek out other members of your department or team, but don't limit yourself to this group. Start by saying hello—it's as simple as that! Pause at the coffee center to chat about small things. Sit down next to a new person in the lunchroom. Ask people about their work, family, or other interests—usually people are pleased to have someone interested in them.

Individual entrepreneurs and home-office workers can make the effort to get together as a group to form a community and share their experiences—successes and problems, worries and concerns. Weekly or monthly gatherings (even Internet chat rooms) with the express purpose of connection are primarily used as professional networking tools, but they can also fulfill a human need for connectedness.

Connectedness to a mission On the job, caring about your team's projects or your company's mission can help you feel just as connected as sharing news with a colleague. Feeling as if you are a part of the whole, not just some interchangeable peg, gives you a sense of your own worth. As a supervisor, encouraging this kind of connected spirit will increase your team's productivity. As an employee, caring can help turn negative worry into positive energy.

Together, these two kinds of connectedness can produce a sense of community in the workplace that is essential for the well-being and productivity of all of its members.

Achieving quick-fix connections

Long-term positive and trusting relationships may be the best kind of anti-worry connection, but there are times when a person simply needs a quick fix. Quick-fix connections don't solve deeper problems, but they can be very useful for those occasional crises that almost everyone experiences. Reassurance and venting are two tools for achieving quick-fix connections.

Reassurance as a bandage If, for example, two different supervisors ask one employee for two separate reports due on the same day, the employee may feel panicked, overwhelmed by the enormity of the required tasks. The work may seem impossible, and anticipating failure can set off waves of toxic stress. What to do? In this situation, the employee could use some reassurance just to help make it through this tough time.

Reassurance is a type of connectedness that says to the worrier that everything will be fine. It's a kind of comfort that can soothe

the anxious mind with a counteracting voice and offer just enough encouragement to help the worrier get through the difficult time. It's easy to give and warmly received.

- **Getting reassurance.** When you need reassurance, ask for it. That's difficult for some people, but it's worth learning how to do it. Don't make someone guess from your body language or roundabout questions that you need reassurance. Just say, "Tell me everything is going to be okay." But even more important, ask the right person. Some people simply can't respond—they may be too distant or too honest. Make sure the person you ask knows when to be reassuring and when to provide his or her honest opinion.

- **Giving reassurance.** Even though it's easy to give reassurance, it may seem hard. If you've never received it yourself, if you believe a person needs to be "strong" enough to make it through without reassurance, or if you believe you always need to be honest about the prospects of success or failure, you may resist giving reassurance. However, you may be pleasantly surprised at how a little reassurance can go a long way toward turning an anxious person into a more productive one. Say the words, "It'll be fine." Give a pat on the back, a little hug, a bit of hope to build some confidence.

The problem with reassurance is that it is just a bandage used to cover a hurt. If it's the only tool used to counteract worry, it's not enough. Chronic worriers need much more than just reassurance; chronic worriers need to challenge themselves in more systematic and holistic ways.

Tip: When giving reassurance, use body language to show your concern—a person under stress wants to be heard on all levels. Make eye contact with and lean toward the speaker. Nod your head to show you understand. Use facial expressions to indicate feelings.

Venting as relief Another kind of quick-fix connection is venting. If, for example, you have a bad week when everything seems to go wrong—your car breaks down, your assistant quits, your computer gets a virus, your budget request is denied—you can feel overwhelmed and begin to wonder what new catastrophe awaits. The stress of dealing with these real problems can suddenly escalate and interfere with a rational approach to problem solving. That's when not only reassurance but also a healthy session of venting can help.

Venting can offer relief by allowing you to unburden your problems. Just listing them out loud can diminish their power to assault your worried mind. Venting can be good for you! But be sure to vent to the right person. You need someone who will listen and sympathize, not someone who will brush aside your list as unimportant, and not someone who wants to solve everything for you. The purpose of venting is to ease your mind, giving you the mental space to return to the problems with renewed energy to deal with them as needed.

? What You COULD Do.

Remember Ellen and her desire to feel less vulnerable?

Ellen is correct in seeing feelings of vulnerability for what they are: a major part of the worry equation (vulnerability + powerlessness = worry). She could reduce her feelings of vulnerability through two means. First, she could connect with colleagues, perhaps by systematically scheduling lunches and other social interactions with members of her department and people from other departments. Connecting with others is actually a powerful antidote to stress and worry because it eases feelings of isolation and therefore vulnerability. By interacting with others, Ellen can also conduct reality checks on her concerns, as well as share news, ideas, and resources. She may discover she's not alone in her struggle to manage stress.

Ellen could also remind herself that she has consistently done a good job and that her supervisor has given her positive performance reviews. When people are stressed, they tend to engage in negative self-talk—such as overgeneralizing or blaming themselves inappropriately for problems. By replacing such thought patterns with more positive self-talk, Ellen can reframe the way

(continued)

she perceives stressful events and reduce her feelings of vulnerability. For example, if she were to ask her supervisor if he expects her to present the usual reports at the next meeting, she may learn that he does—and that her colleague was actually talking about a possible new *format* for the printed reports.

Connecting with Yourself

Using self-talk

Connecting with yourself may be one of the most effective strategies for challenging stress and winning. As we grow up and learn about the world around us, we develop automatic thoughts to help us sort through our perceptions and experiences. If these automatic thoughts are healthy and constructive, we cope with our life in positive ways. However, chronic worriers often subject themselves to negative automatic thoughts that contribute to their worry and stress.

Eroding the destructive power of negative thoughts

Negative self-talk, what you say to yourself, contributes directly to your stress. Self-talk is related to your internal assumptions and beliefs, and it is typically automatic, familiar, and unconscious. For example, our bodies can't sort out the experiences we have from the events we imagine. As we imagine a bad outcome—say, being fired from a job—our bodies react to the thought as though it were actually happening. All the physical reactions that would occur in a dangerous situation will occur in an imagined one, too.

Also, we talk to ourselves constantly, and if those messages are negative and critical ("How could I do such a foolish thing!") or name-calling ("I'm an idiot!")—we start to believe them. Finally, we rarely stop to consider what we are saying to ourselves. We don't counter the criticisms, for example, with understanding or forgiveness. In other words, we don't test our own assumptions. Because we don't counter negative thoughts—such as, "I know I won't get that raise"—those thoughts can become self-fulfilling.

Tuning in to your self-talk

To accurately tune into your negative self-talk, you must first identify your automatic thoughts. These are spontaneous thoughts that may or may not reflect the reality of your situation.

To begin, think about what you tell yourself when you first arrive at the office in the morning. Is the message positive or negative? Is there a familiar feel to the message? For example, do you see your desk and think, "I'll never get everything done today"? If so, is this message accurate? Could you be distorting or exaggerating the situation?

Identifying and avoiding common mind traps

Automatic thoughts often fall into categories called *mind traps*. These mind traps are irrational beliefs that can lead you astray from a clear and realistic perception of your world. Identifying the ones you use and are comfortable with will help you challenge them. Consider how your automatic thinking might fall into the traps listed in the table, "About mind traps."

About mind traps

Mind traps	What they are
"Should" statements	"I should do this. I must do that." You motivate yourself with "shoulds" and then feel guilty.
All-or-nothing thinking	"One mistake, and total failure will result." You see things in extremes of black or white, all bad or all good.
Overgeneralizations	"This always happens." You set a pattern of inevitability to an event that happens once or twice.
Mental filtering	"This one mistake ruins everything." You see only the negative side to an event and ignore the positive one.
Rejection of positive experiences	"The team complimented my work just to be polite." You accept only the negative messages.
Jumping to conclusions	"Our department is being restructured. I know I'll be fired." Without bothering to get the facts, you assume the worst.
Emotional reasoning	"I feel like a loser, so I must be a loser." You assume your negative feelings represent reality.
Labeling	"I'm so stupid and irresponsible to be late for that meeting!" You label yourself negatively.
Personalizing	"The proposal was rejected because I was on the team." You assign cause and blame to yourself inappropriately.

Challenging self-talk distortions

Once you can identify the mind traps that you easily fall into, begin to challenge them, one by one. The table, "Mind-trap remedies" offers possible remedies for common mind traps.

Mind-trap remedies

Mind traps	Remedies
"Should" statements	Use the verb "want" instead of "should." Give yourself some flexibility in deciding what you want to do.
All-or-nothing thinking	Don't make black-or-white judgments. Think of the in-between points or percentages (for example, 40% or 75%).
Overgeneralizations	Examine the evidence. Is something always true? Or has it happened two times out of the past five?
Mental filtering	Look for the positive side as well as the negative. Focus on solving the problem.
Rejection of positive experiences	Acknowledge and accept the reality of positive experiences or events.
Jumping to conclusions	Get the facts first. See if the evidence supports your conclusion.
Emotional reasoning	Step away from just your emotions, and try to look at yourself as others see you.
Labeling	Describe the behavior, not yourself. If you make a mistake, acknowledge the mistake; don't blame yourself.
Personalizing	Make yourself prove that you are responsible for the situation. What is the evidence?

Choosing positive self-talk

Choosing positive self-talk over existing mind traps isn't easy. However, adopting a positive outlook is critical to avoiding workplace stress. To reprogram your self-talk, start slowly. Consider how you can reframe the way you perceive events. Reframing is a way of restating negative self-talk into positive affirmation. It puts the picture or experience into a different frame, so that you can look at it in a new way. Consider the worst-case scenario of a given situation. For example, what if you do get fired after a merger? What would happen to you? What new opportunities might emerge from that event? In other words, look at a situation from as many different views as possible. What can you learn about it? A situation that might seem disastrous could offer exciting new opportunities. What seems like a terrible mistake may be a great chance to learn.

Also think about how you can affirm yourself. Give yourself reassurance and support. Positive and constructive self-talking takes practice; at first, it may seem uncomfortable. But keep on doing it. Tell yourself that you're fine, that you'll make it, and that you deserve that raise. Give yourself credit when it's due. The positive alternatives will gain strength because they actually make more sense.

REFRAMING *v* **1:** restating destructive self-talk into positive ways of perceiving events

Letting Your Body Help You Relieve Stress

Understanding stress's impact on the body

There are times when no matter how much you evaluate, plan, and remediate, no matter how connected you become to others and to your own feelings, you may still be burdened by those real situations that deserve your attention and concern. Or you may still feel those waves of anxiety and stress in spite of how thoughtful, analytical, or connected you may be. One important way to manage your stress, whatever its source, is to exercise your body. Changing your physical state can help change your mental state.

After all, stress has a direct impact on your body. In the short term, it gives you that energy surge and alertness you need to confront a threatening situation. However, prolonged stress puts an unhealthy strain on your body. Prolonged stress can:

- Raise your cholesterol level

- Cause your arteries to restrict, limiting blood flow to the heart

- Disrupt your digestive process and result in stomach acid, constipation, diarrhea, ulcers, or even cancer of the bowels

- Stimulate migraine headaches, asthma attacks, or other allergic reactions

Committing to exercise

The easiest, cheapest, and most natural antidote to worry is exercise. Exercise benefits your brain by:

- Reducing tension

- Easing aggression and frustration

- Providing an increased sense of well-being

- Improving sleep

- Aiding concentration

Exercise is also good for almost every other part of your body—heart, circulation, bones, respiratory system, skin, and so on. And it helps you reduce your weight, lower your blood pressure, and regulate your blood sugar.

Worry tends to put your body in a frozen, unmoving state. Exercise helps you break out of the immobility. So start by simply moving. Rock and sway. Get up and stretch. Even better, take a walk or climb some stairs. Even those brief physical efforts can help clear your mind of the weight of worry.

Better yet, get in the habit of exercising on a regular basis— three to four times a week, if possible. Choose something you enjoy doing—walking, running, bicycling, inline skating, hiking, swimming, rowing, playing tennis or basketball. If you don't enjoy it, you won't keep it up.

Eating healthfully

Eating is another way to cope with stress. If you consume junk food as a response to a stressful day, food has become a negative coping response for you. But if you eat a healthy and varied diet, your body will be better able to deal with the normal or higher levels of stress you face each day.

Some ways to achieve healthy eating habits include those listed here.

- **Maintain a healthy weight.** Toxic stress can affect your weight by causing you to under- or overeat. Either way, your body won't have the optimum level of energy it needs to function effectively. First, determine the healthiest body weight for you, taking into account that this number varies by height, gender, and age. Then, if you do need to adjust your body weight, choose a slow, steady weight-loss or -gain diet.

- **Eat a variety of food.** Not only is it more interesting to vary your diet, but you also give your body the full range of nutrients it needs. Eating plenty of vegetables, fruit, and grains is especially healthy.

- **Reduce the level of fat and cholesterol in your diet.** Eat foods that are broiled, baked, or steamed rather than fried. Limit your intake of animal products such as egg yolks.

- **Moderate your consumption of alcohol and caffeine.** Alcohol is a depressant and can disturb your sleep, which only worsens stress. Caffeine is a stimulant and can amplify feelings of nervousness.

Sleeping restfully

Insomnia can be caused by stress, and lack of sleep can aggravate the level of stress. This can cause you to become more tense, irritable, and anxious. People vary in the amount of sleep they need, but your body will tell you what's right for you. Pay attention to how you feel in the morning after more or less sleep. Then make an effort to get the amount of sleep that's right for you. If you are having problems sleeping, try some of these simple sleep-improving activities.

- **Reduce your intake of caffeinated beverages and alcohol.** These substances tend to disrupt your sleep.

- **Exercise regularly.** You'll burn off tension from the day and more easily clear your mind before going to bed.

- **Plan the next day's activities early in the evening.** You'll give yourself time to clear your head before going to bed.

- **Make your sleeping environment as quiet and dark as possible.** Quiet and darkness are especially conducive to sound sleep.

- **Establish a routine for going to sleep.** For example, if you get into the habit of having a warm glass of milk or reading for half an hour before drifting off to sleep, these behaviors will eventually serve as strong signals that it's time to sleep.

- **Use relaxation techniques to help yourself fall asleep.** For example, some people find it helpful to count backward from 25, 50, or 100. Others imagine each set of muscles melting like butter.

- **If you can't sleep, get out of bed and do something soothing until you feel sleepy again.** Lying in bed and trying your hardest to fall asleep will only lead to frustration.

"There is more to life than just increasing its speed."
—Mahatma Gandhi

Mastering the relaxation response

The relaxation response is a structured approach to using breathing and relaxation to counter the negative effects of stress. It is a deliberate and controlled technique that is opposite to the body's natural fight-or-flight stress response in the face of apparent danger or a perceived threatening situation. While the body's fight-or-flight mode causes an increase in the heart rate and breathing, the relaxation response reverses these bodily states.

When you find yourself feeling unnecessary stress, apply this simple technique to counteract the negative effects of stress on your body. To prepare, you will need:

- **A quiet environment.** Find a quiet, calm place; a private room; or a space with no distractions.

- **A mental device.** Choose a constant stimulus of a single-syllable sound or word, such as the word *one*. Repeat that sound silently or softly over and over again. Focus solely on that sound.

- **A passive attitude.** Disregard all distracting thoughts. Simply let yourself be completely passive.

- **A comfortable position.** Sit in a comfortable chair, preferably with neck and head support. Loosen all tight-fitting clothes. Prop your feet up, if possible.

To induce the relaxation response, follow these steps.

1. Sit in a comfortable position.

2. Close your eyes.

3. Deeply relax your muscles, starting with your toes and moving up to your face and head.

4. Breathe through your nose. As you breathe out, say the sound or word you have chosen silently or softly to yourself. Breathe in. Breathe out and say the word again. Breathe in.

5. Keep repeating the breathing pattern and the sound for 20 minutes. Open your eyes to check the time, but do not use an alarm or other sharp noise.

6. When you finish, sit quietly for several minutes, at first with your eyes closed and then with your eyes open.

After using this technique, most people feel calm and relaxed, but perhaps the most important benefit is an immediate lowering of blood pressure. And the interruption of stressful and worried thoughts can enable you to focus more clearly on the real situation.

Tip: Relax whenever and wherever you can. Practice relaxation techniques whenever you start to feel the first signs of tension, worry, or stress. While quick exercises that you can do almost anywhere are helpful, find the time and space for longer, more meditative relaxation—these exercises are more beneficial in the long run.

Practicing Good Stress Habits

Avoiding stress stimulants

Stress stimulants surround us in our busy, modern world. Try to avoid those superficial stress arousers and focus on only those matters that are truly important. For example, *shun negative office politics and workplace conflicts.* Intra- and interdepartmental rivalries can create an artificial sense of competition and crisis. Genuine teamwork and shared activities create a more effective and productive environment. If you have the power to move your colleagues away from conflict and toward a connected community, you will be helping not only yourself but the organization as well.

Also *limit excessive media stimulants.* Too much Internet time can aggravate tension due to the flashing advertisements, overly busy pages, frustratingly slow downloads, and startling pop-up menus. Skip exaggerated disaster news stories; one of their purposes is to arouse your level of worry. Avoid watching too much television—it's another source of extraneous information and pressure.

Finally, *restrict your intake of caffeinated beverages, alcohol, and sugar.* They may seem to help give you what you want at the moment—whether it's being alert with caffeine, or gaining a quick energy pick-me-up with sugar, or relaxing with an alcoholic drink—but these effects are all superficial. Overuse can produce the opposite effect.

Adopting stress busters

Incorporate stress busters into your everyday routine to help you deal with those moments when your body tenses up at the thought of another long budget meeting, at the message you received from your supervisor to see him immediately, or at the workaholic's announcement that she worked all weekend. Stress busters can become easy and natural ways to help you endure those anxious moments and enjoy your life and work.

Try "minis"   Minis are shorter versions of the relaxation response technique that you can use quickly whenever you feel tension beginning to grip you. Taking the following actions will help to reduce stress if you don't have a lot of time.

- Take a deep breath and hold it for several seconds. Then let your breath out very slowly while repeating your focus word.

- Put your right hand just under your navel. Focus on breathing down to your navel. As you breathe in the first time, say the number *ten*. Breathe out. Then breathe in and say the number *nine*. Breathe out. Continue until you reach *zero*.

- Breathe in through your nose and breathe out through your mouth ten times. Notice how cool the air feels when you inhale and how warm it is when you exhale.

- Imagine air as a cloud. As you breathe, envision that the air comes to you as a cloud, filling you and then leaving you.

Enjoy humor Laughing can transform that rigidly tight facial expression of tension into more relaxed and flexible features. Humor is also a way to reframe negative self-talk into something more positive and fun.

Step back from the worry and strain of the job, and look for the funny side of things.

- Find the humor in everyday situations. Watch out for coincidences, ironies, and contradictions.

- Think about playing at your work. Many routine tasks can be seen as game-playing moves.

- Collect cartoons to decorate your workspace.

- Exaggerate something to the point of absurdity. Step out of your usual bounds, or say the unexpected occasionally.

- Take your standard negative self-talk lines, and rephrase them into funny talk. For example, change "This always happens to me" to "And I only volunteer 60% of the time!"

NOTE: Don't mistake humor for ridicule. Laughing at someone or at the expense of someone is not nearly as funny as it is hurtful. Real humor is based on respect and includes everyone in the fun.

Take a break Our bodies and minds need time-outs, breaks from our work and activities. Pay attention to your stress and energy levels. When you feel tension rising and energy falling, take a break. Some stress-reducing changes in your work pattern include:

- Listening to music
- Going for a walk
- Chatting with friends
- Climbing some stairs

These are brief, daily breaks. Be sure to schedule longer breaks such as extended weekends or short getaways as well. Ride out into the country, stay in a bed-and-breakfast, go hiking or fishing, or simply read a good book. A complete and longer change of pace can help you perceive your work world in a whole new way—with less worry and more energy.

All of these activities can reduce stress and restore energy. Moments of leisure, relaxation, and pleasure mean less worry and dis-stress.

Managing Time

How to Look at the Big Picture

Dost thou love life? Then do
not squander time, for that's the stuff life is made of.
—Benjamin Franklin

Time—it's a resource that we can't buy or sell, share with others or take from them, get more of or have less of. Every day, each of us has the same amount of time—24 hours. It's what we do with it that makes a difference. The people who make the most of their time may apply different techniques and systems, but they all have one thing in common. They have a vision of how they want to spend their time, a vision that includes a clear sense of priorities. They know what they want to do with their time.

Peter Wakeman and his wife, Laura, founded the Great Harvest Bread Company 25 years ago. As entrepreneurs, it would have been easy to allow their work to consume every moment of their lives. But they had a vision of how they would spend their time, and one priority was clear from the beginning: They would not work on weekends and they would take a vacation every year.

"In the early days of the business we had simple rules, but we followed them like a religion. One was the two-day weekend. We never violated that, no matter what—it was a line we were afraid to cross, as though lightning would strike us down if we did."

—Pete Wakeman, owner
  Great Harvest Bread Company

Since then, the Great Harvest Bread Company has grown to a chain of 137 franchises. Their priority of having personal time drove Pete and Laura to grow their business in a very conscious way. For a pair of successful business owners, Pete and Laura take a surprising amount of time off from work. It's all done with a rigorous attention to leveraging time.

"We really like strong lines between things. We carry time cards, and we punch in, punch out, to the nearest five minutes. We know when we're working. . . . I have a little Excel sheet I keep, and we make a conscious decision each year how many hours we will work. . . . In 1996 we decided to go to 1,000 hours each, basically half-time. . . . Aside from the 1,000-hour rule, we vary our schedule any way we want."

—Pete Wakeman

TIME LEVERAGING *n* 1: spending your time wisely on activities that move you closer to your goals. 2: the process of assessing and planning how to use your time to accomplish your goals.

What's the value of leveraging your time?

Whatever your priority is—whether it's personal time, as it is for Pete and Laura, or another goal such as increasing sales, developing a new product, writing a business plan, or completing a project—leveraging time can help you achieve it.

What's the difference between leveraging your time and managing it? Leveraging time is a strategy of using time in an intelligent way to pursue your most important goals. Managing time is the day-to-day process you use to leverage the time—the scheduling, the to-do lists, the delegating, and other systems that help you use time efficiently. Without the strategy—the vision and the plan—time management won't necessarily help you achieve your goals. That's why the first step in leveraging your time is to clarify your priorities.

Why do we do what we do?

Most of us have schedules that we follow, deadlines we meet, tasks we achieve efficiently and competently every day. But why? *Why* do we do the things that we do? *How* do our activities and accomplishments get us closer to our professional and personal goals? Try answering these questions:

- Are you using your time to accomplish the things you truly want?

- Are you simply running in place?

- Are you somewhere in between—moving forward, but slowly and uncertainly?

If you're not using your time to pursue your most important goals, then it's time to change.

Look strategically at the big picture

Time leveraging means looking strategically at how to spend your time. It means making sure you are spending time in the right places—on the things that are most important to you. It means allocating your time so you get the biggest return for the time spent.

For example:

- Do you get more leverage from doing work yourself or from training a team of others?

- Do you get more leverage from reading manuals to learn a new skill or from a few intensive and structured learning sessions?

- Do you get more leverage from your team with an open-door policy or offering support for team solutions?

Simply put, to avoid "running in place," make sure you are leveraging your time appropriately.

How to Audit
Your Time

I deally, everything you do should be valuable for you—valuable in terms of actively moving toward your professional or personal goals—the things *you* want to achieve. No one else can make these decisions for you. You have to decide what's important to and for you.

Create a big-picture vision of where you want to be

In this section, you'll learn how to conduct a *Baseline Time-Management Audit* and create a *Current Time Allocation Pie Chart.* You'll then create a *Target Allocation Pie Chart.*

The first phase in leveraging your time is to assess how you are currently spending your time. Although conducting a time audit may seem like busywork, it's actually an important first step in leveraging time. In order to spend time effectively, you need an accurate picture of how you are spending your time now. This information about what you're really doing will help you to create a picture that shows you where you want to be. You'll determine how what you *are* doing relates to what you *want* to or *should* do. As you look at how you are spending your time now, your goals will come into focus more clearly.

Break down your work into goal-related categories

Here are some typical categories that most managers spend their time on. You may find that your categories differ from these, but the general process of identifying them remains the same.

- **Growth and improvement.** This category focuses on *opportunities*, not crises. It's often the one in which the added value you bring to your unit or company is the greatest. For a product manager, it's the time spent innovating; for an operations manager, it's the time spent improving processes; for the senior executive, it's the time spent on strategy.

- **Managing people.** You may want to break this down into three smaller goals: 1) managing up, 2) managing across, and 3) managing down. Coaching and mentoring direct reports or a team enable you to use your time better, but you must also cultivate lateral and upward relationships in order to be successful. Effective leaders understand that time spent cultivating upward and lateral relationships is high-leverage time that can help you move toward your goals.

- **Nonmanagerial responsibilities.** Most managers have day-to-day responsibilities beyond managing people. For a project manager, it means tracking schedules and budgets and dealing with vendors. For an architect, it may be designing a building. For a software developer, it may mean writing code, or checking everyone else's. Whatever your job, these are the ongoing, daily activities that can be defined as "business as usual."

What Would YOU Do?

The Fun House

Daniel was giddy after his promotion. He knew his new responsibilities would be challenging, but he hadn't expected to lose control completely. Buffeted about the company by others, dragged in and out of meetings by his boss, his peers, and his direct reports, Daniel's head was spinning. The pile on his desk grew and grew. And every time he'd pull something out of the pile to work on it, someone would need him to do something ASAP, or the phone would start ringing, or an e-mail would pop up on his screen, or another meeting would start.

One evening, he was alone in his office. No people. No phone. No e-mails. Just Daniel and the big pile. He didn't even know where to begin. At the top? That stuff might be the most important. At the bottom? That stuff had been around the longest. Daniel sighed. How had he come to this? He'd been a terrific worker, gotten everything done efficiently and on time, really enjoyed his work. Why was he so out of control as a manager? How could he figure out where to focus his energy? How could he regain control over his own day?

What would YOU do? See *What You COULD Do.*

- **Administration.** Administration includes such necessary chores as assessing your department's resource needs, interviewing job candidates, responding to letters and e-mails, filling out time sheets and expense reports, and writing performance evaluations. This is the category that shocks most people when they do their time audit. Administrative tasks tend to consume great amounts of time.

Audit your time for one week

Carefully examine and record the time you spend on each activity over the course of one week. This one-week time-management assessment gives you a snapshot of how you actually spend your time. Keeping track of your hours for a week is not difficult, and the results are often surprising.

"The last time I kept a log, I was surprised to learn that when I am in the office, I spend almost half my time on the telephone, either taking calls or leaving messages for people who aren't available."

—Elaine Biech,
The Consultant's Quick Start Guide

Focus on your most important activities. Rather than covering all your activities, you may want to conduct a single goal audit in a category that is particularly important for you.

For example, Beth Chapman, engagement manager for a health-care consulting services group, was sure that she was spending too much time on administrative tasks, so she audited the time she spent in that area for a week.

"Since I travel a lot, I have to do a lot of expense reports. I kept a really accurate record of every minute I spent doing expense reports. At the end of a week, I documented that I had spent four hours on expense reports—that's half a day! When I saw the actual numbers, even I was surprised. Then I made a case to my supervisor that a half day of my time with our customers during a one-week period was a lot more valuable to the company than a half day of my time filling out expense reports."

—Beth Chapman,
engagement manager

Audit your *personal* time as well as your work time. Time management is not just about working more efficiently and getting more done. Time management is a valuable tool that can help you achieve balance in your life. To get the *whole* picture, as well as the *big* picture, audit the time you spend away from work on a separate chart.

Leverage your time to achieve your desired lifestyle. For example, when Elisabeth Choi, an equity analyst and mother of two preschoolers, decided to reduce her workweek from 40 to 30 hours, she found that fixed schedules helped her use her time effectively so she could do the things she wanted to do.

"You want to watch your kids grow up, do yoga, exercise, and work in the garden. When I started working part-time, I began to use a fixed schedule. For example, every Tuesday morning I go shopping. The supermarket is empty then, so it's very efficient. I also learned how long things really took. Once you have a handle on what has to get done and how long those things take, then the rest is free time.

The more you can organize your time, the more time you have to do the things you want to do. It's why you decided not to be out there working full-time and going crazy."

—Elisabeth Choi,
   equity analyst

Steps to Auditing Your Time

To audit the time you spend at work:

1. Create a chart like the one shown on the next page. List the days of the week down the rows. Across the top of the columns, list the major goal-related categories that you spend time pursuing.
2. After you complete an activity, record the time you spent under the related category. For example, after a one-hour sales call, enter the time under the "sales" category.
3. At the end of the day, and at the end of the week, add the total hours spent on each category.
4. Analyze your audit. Divide the total time spent on each goal into the total time spent at work. Translate these numbers into percentages, as shown below.
5. Create a pie chart that visually shows how you have spent your time during the past week.
6. After examining the results of your audit, ask yourself, "Is this how I want to be spending my time?"

The sample chart (Baseline Time-Management Audit Tool) on the following page shows the results of a time audit, including the percentage breakdown shown in the bottom row.

(continued)

BASELINE TIME-MANAGEMENT AUDIT TOOL

Week Ending: (04/02)	Activity: Sales	Activity: Customer Management	Activity: Team Management	Activity: Strategic Planning	Activity: Managing Up	Activity: Administration	Total Time/Day:
Monday	2 hrs	1 hr	3 hrs	O hrs	O hrs	2 hrs	8 hrs
Tuesday	3	1	4	O	O	2	10
Wednesday	7	O	O	O	1	2	10
Thursday	O	3	3	O	O	2	8
Friday	1	2	O	3	1	2	9
Total Time / Activity	13 hrs	7 hrs	10 hrs	3 hrs	2 hrs	10 hrs	44 hrs
% of Time	29%	16%	22%	7%	4%	22%	100%

Tip: Use a calendar or a PDA to track your time—whatever is most convenient.

What You COULD Do.

Let's go back to Daniel's problem.

The spinning-head syndrome Daniel is experiencing can often accompany a promotion into management. But he can catch his breath by taking these three steps:

1. Daniel needs to slow down and start thinking about leveraging and managing his time. First, he needs to determine what his new job entails and break his responsibilities into key goals. Once the goals are clear, he can then figure out what his priorities are in each area. He may need to seek the advice of his supervisor and get input on what is expected of him so he can determine what is, and what isn't, a priority.

2. Once Daniel has a clear picture of how he should be spending his time, he can then start to assess how well he is managing his time. To do this, Daniel could start tracking his time to determine what tasks are steering him off track. This will also help Daniel estimate how long things will actually take to complete, allowing him to plan more accurately in the future. By going through this exercise, Daniel can work with his supervisor to continue to shape his role and get the help he needs, whether it's an assistant or delegating tasks to others.

(continued)

Daniel will most likely also have to start being a bit more disciplined when it comes to sharing his time. If Daniel is respectful of his own time, he will find that others will begin to respect it as well.

3. As for that pile of papers, the first thing Daniel needs to do is skim the pile and organize the material into three smaller (and more manageable) piles:

   - Must-do (that is, meeting a deadline or satisfying an important person)
   - Can-wait
   - Easy-to-knock-off

He can start with the Must-do pile. Then, because it helps build confidence, he can tend to the Easy-to-knock-off pile just to get the work down to a less overwhelming size. Once the Easy-to-knock-off and Must-do piles are out of the way and when small blocks of unexpected time open up, he can deal with the Can-waits.

Compare your audit results to your goals

Once you have an idea of how you spend your time, review your time-audit charts with your supervisor. If you are expected to drive the planning process, but you are currently spending 80% of your time supervising others, your time audit can help you set the stage for an objective, meaningful discussion about your role and what you should be doing.

How to Develop Your Plan

You've identified your major goals, key activities, and associated tasks. The next step in leveraging your time is to make sure your overall plan is realistic and attainable. Put all your high-priority categories and activities together into a Time Leverage Plan and allot time by percent of total time available. How does this percentage translate into actual hours in a 40-hour week? Can you perform the tasks within the given amount of time? (See the table, Time-Leveraging Plan Tool, on the next page.)

Another way to look at the picture is with a pie chart that quickly shows which category should be receiving most of your time and attention.

Once you've created a *Target Time Allocation* pie chart (see figure 1), compare it to your *Actual Time Allocation* chart (see figure 2). How are they different? What can you learn from them?

"Your time audit is important. Your vision of where you should be putting your time—and why—is important. But you need to be proactive. You can't just go in to your supervisor and say, 'Oh, look at this. Do something about it.' *You need to present realistic ways to solve the problem, and you need to push to get the resources you need so you can do the job that you were hired to do. Your time audit and your vision of where you want to go are tools that can help you get there."*

—Beth Chapman

Week

Goal-related Category	What does success look like? How will I know if I am successful?	% Time Required	Hours/ Workweek	Key Activities
Sales	Close 3 new accounts per month.	30%	12	• Make two sales calls a week. • Research new leads. • Write sales reports. • Submit bids.
Customer Management	Ensure smooth transition from sales to production.	10%	4	• Attend kick-off meetings. • Follow-up with phone calls.
Team Management	• Allot time to meet with staff. • Plan training program for new hires.	20%	8	• One-hour weekly meetings with each rep. Two weekly meetings with team. • Contact Human Resources about new-hire training.
Strategic Planning	Develop new annual strategy.	20%	8	• Draft plan. • Review plan with Joe.
Managing Up	• Keep CEO updated. • Get input from upper management on strategic plan.	5%	2	• Make appointment to meet with CEO. • Arrange two meetings with upper management.
Administration	Expense reports, e-mails, etc.	5%	2	• Deal with e-mails. • Review expense reports. • Process invoices.
Other	Contingency time	10%	4	
		100%	40	

Reality-check your actual and target time allocations

When you look at the time it will realistically take to achieve your goals, you may quickly realize that you could end up working 150 hours a week. Everybody needs more time. But since nobody gets more than 24 hours a day, your only choice is to use time more effectively.

FIGURE 1

Actual time allocation

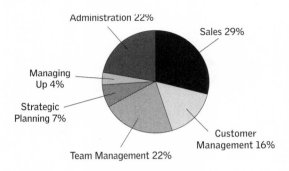

FIGURE 2

Target time allocation

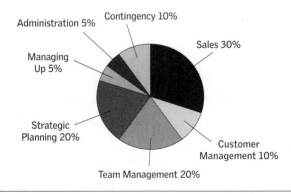

One way to carve out the time you need to pursue your goals is to reduce the time you spend on other activities. But how?

If you've done a time audit of your low-priority activities, you're probably aware of the areas you wish to spend less time on. Now compare the actual time you spend each week with your big-picture time allotment to get a more concrete idea of where and by how much you need to reduce your time.

For example, say you want to reduce by 15% the time you spend on administrative chores—time that could then be transferred to strategic planning and managing up. For most managers, reducing time spent on administrative chores by 15% may be an unrealistic immediate goal, but any steps you take in a positive direction will get you on track.

"Something I've done since high school is make lists. I go out as far as a week. I print out an Outlook calendar for the week. I try to approximate how long things will take and I make lists of phone calls, projects, or other things I want to accomplish that week. By the end of the week, I will have knocked off a bunch of things. I find that in addition to scheduling my time, it just helps me remember what I have to do."
—Elisabeth Choi

How to Time-Box

everaging your time takes dedication and persistence, but it pays off when you finally take your plan and put it into action—by managing your time! The key activities in your Time Leverage Plan become your to-do list, making the plan a reality. Some people may start with a "big vision" plan that incorporates all their major goals. Others may feel more comfortable and satisfied by targeting one key goal and starting to work toward it first. Whichever way you start, making a schedule and trying your best to stick to it is an effecttive way of getting there. How can you do this? Try time-boxing.

Time-box a realistic schedule

Time-boxing is a powerful scheduling method that can help you block out your days. With a vision of your big-picture time allocation and task-oriented to-do list to accomplish, you can start to box your time into a manageable schedule like the one shown on page 154. Give yourself a little extra time in your estimates. You're more likely to underestimate than to overestimate how long a task will take. In other words, build in unscheduled time to handle the unexpected.

How to time-box

Simply put, time-boxing is an iterative process that helps you shape your schedule to accomplish your desired goals.

Create a to-do list. Decide what you want to accomplish, and then create a to-do list of tasks. List everything you want to accomplish in a given time period—a day, week, month, or quarter. The to-do list can include goals, tasks necessary to achieve the goals, and personal activities such as exercise.

Break your list into categories. Take your to-do list and organize it by breaking it into categories. Group your tasks by job functions such as strategy, business development, daily operations, and people management. (Remember: the time-boxing technique can be applied to your personal life as well—group a personal to-do list into categories such as gardening, playing golf, or cooking.)

Record your time. For one week, keep a record of what you do and how long each task takes. Track your accomplishments, noting what you finish, what you don't finish. At the end of the week, look back at your record to see if you're spending your time in the right places, the places you feel are important.

Build your time-estimating skill. If you don't set parameters for how much time to devote to each task, to-do lists will only be marginally useful. Estimate how much time you think each item on the list will require. Estimating will not only help you complete the items on your list, but it will improve your ability to estimate time

What Would YOU Do?

Running in Place

arisol went through her pile of "to-do" lists, checking off item after item. Done, done, done, done, done. With each flick of the felt tip, one more task was lifted from her shoulders. Then she copied the tasks that remained onto a new list.

To Do

- Write report for next week.
- Hire new person to replace Tom.
- Meet with Mark to come up with budget for Lawrence bid.

She paused in dismay. These were all the most critical priorities! What had she been doing when she should have been completing these tasks? She glanced at her schedule.

Yesterday there was that meeting with Tony that she really didn't have to go to. Then she and Shelly spent the rest of the morning discussing the office-supply situation. She had a meeting with Lisa to help her with the sales reports. That took the better part of the afternoon. She had done everything she was supposed to do to use her time better—made schedules and "to-do" lists, screened her calls and returned them all at once—and now every one else was going home, and she hadn't even really started! What was the point of all her careful time management when she still was overworked and frenzied?

What would YOU do?

---

and manage expectations of those around you in the future. Think carefully about all the steps necessary to complete the task; set a realistic estimate. This is the step that *"keeps me honest,"* says Beran Peter, CEO of Arkoa, a technical training services company in Westborough, Massachusetts. *"If I realize I'm not going to hit my estimate, I'm able to assess why and evaluate how I might make a change to get back on track."*

Give yourself some wiggle room. Block off the appropriate amount of time on your calendar for each item. For example, if you estimate that writing a business plan will take 32 hours, you could block off four hours each Tuesday and Thursday morning for the next four weeks. The challenge, of course, is prioritizing and fitting the time in where it makes sense. But don't forget to give yourself some leeway. *Overestimate* rather than underestimate. Change is inevitable, and you may want to add tasks midstream.

Tip: Build in time to delegate and shift the balance
of your time from what you are doing now
to what you should be doing.

As you practice, keep tracking your estimated time against actual time and make adjustments as necessary. Your goal is to manage your day-to-day activities while keeping your big-picture time allocation in mind. (See the Time-Box Tool below.)

TIME-BOX TOOL		
Adapt this to any type of calendar or software program Schedule for Monday and Tuesday mornings		
Time	**Monday**	**Tuesday**
8:00 a.m.	Task: Research strategic plan. Actual time spent:	Task: Research SP; call Joe. Actual time spent:
9:00 a.m.	Task: Monday staff meeting. Actual time spent:	Task: Follow-up on new leads. Actual time spent:
10:00 a.m.	Task: Plan to delegate invoicing task. Actual time spent:	Task: Meet with Joe about his sales figures. Task: Review résumés for administrative assistant position. Actual time spent:
11:00 a.m.	Task: Return phone calls and e-mail messages. Actual time spent:	Task: Work with Jane. Actual time spent:

"*When I want to do something important that doesn't have quite the urgency of, say, an immediate release, I just tell myself I'm just going to spend a half hour each day on it. That's what I do because it will become an emergency if I don't. So each week, on my PDA, I can see if I'm not doing enough future-oriented stuff. I put it on my list and set aside time—every morning from 9:00–9:30—to work on one of those things. It's like practicing the violin.*"

—Michael Rothman,
   software developer

Tip: Why use time-boxing?

- It forces you to think through your daily tasks and to schedule the time necessary to make them happen.

- It provides a framework for setting expectations and boundaries. If your calendar is full, you'll have to say no—or consciously reassess your priorities.

- It improves your ability to estimate time demands. The ability to estimate how long a task will require is a skill that distinguishes seasoned managers.

- You'll be in a better position to assess—and pull the plug on—unproductive initiatives that consume too much time.

What You COULD Do.

Let's go back to Marisol's problem.

Marisol's dilemma is not uncommon. The root cause could be due to a variety of factors such as: not estimating the right amount of time needed to complete the tasks, procrastinating on the most challenging tasks and opting for the quick hits, or the inability to say no to people who demand her time.

While Marisol should work to uncover the root cause of her dilemma, her first tactical step is to take her to-do lists one step further and begin time-boxing the time she needs to complete her priorities. For each item on her to-do list, she needs to list the amount of time she estimates she will need to complete the task. Then, she can block this time off on her calendar (preferably on a visual tool that others can see).

Once this process is complete, she then needs to train herself to manage "the people-side of the equation." When she is approached, she needs to tell people that her time is booked. She can also make some time in her schedule available to others so they can book time around her already-scheduled time blocks.

With flexibility and persistence, you can make the principles of time-boxing work for you!

How to Manage Your Time

everaging your time takes a commitment to using your most valuable asset to achieve your goals. You may decide to plunge in and work on your whole life—work and personal—at once. Or you may decide to proceed incrementally, working on one category or aspect at a time. Whichever path you take, stay on it. You can't leverage your time without implementing a plan. And that is what time management is all about.

Monitor and evaluate your schedule

As your schedule evolves and delegated tasks begin to fall into place, you should be spending more time on the goals you've established. One way to evaluate your progress is to use the checklist on the page 38.

Your schedule is telling you something. Look at your "sometimes" and "never" answers. Ask yourself why you are not making the kind of progress you'd like to see. Is your schedule realistic? Are your own expectations realistic? How about the expectations of others? What is driving you off course? You may be able to use your schedule to discuss your workload with management.

Look at your "always" and "often" answers. How can you build on your progress to make improvement in other areas?

- Do you feel better prepared and focused?

- Can you make reasonable adjustments to your time estimates?

- Are you making measurable progress on achieving your goals?

- Are you scheduling too many activities?

Tip: Stay focused on your goals. Try to commit to tasks that support your goals. You may be tempted to commit to a task outside of your stated goals to be a team player, but agree to do it only if it does not jeopardize your other work. Learn to say no—diplomatically, of course—to nonpriority projects.

How can you reduce time spent on low-priority activities? Delegate!

Managers are often afraid to delegate, even when they have the resources to do it. But micromanaging can hold you back from achieving your goals, whether those goals are professional or personal.

For example, when Pete and Laura Wakeman, founders of the Great Harvest Bread Company, take off for three-week backpacking trips in the wilderness, they leave their people completely in charge. Pete Wakeman says that delegating is the only way it's possible for them to take a vacation.

"Trust your people, even if they don't solve the problems exactly the same way you do. Problems that may seem to be over their heads usually aren't, and they'll have a much more interesting summer if things are not running like clockwork."
—Pete Wakeman

CHECKLIST FOR EVALUATING YOUR SCHEDULE

	Always	Often	Sometimes	Never
Are you making measurable progress on achieving your goals?			✓	
Do you feel more prepared and focused?		✓		
Are you completing the tasks you set for the week?				✓
Do you have realistic plans for completing tasks you have not finished?		✓		
Are you scheduling approximately the right number of activities?			✓	
Are your time estimates becoming more accurate?	✓			
Can you reduce any activities or tasks that do not support your high-priority tasks?			✓	

Once you've decided what tasks to delegate and you've made the duties involved in that task clear, you have to step back—or forward. For Pete, this literally means putting one foot in front of the other.

"Remember the power of the physical solution: Physically put one foot in front of the other (and I mean your physical foot), and you'll find your physical body moving out the door. Your brain may object vigorously, but it has to go, physically, where your body carries it. Then, physically, don't look back. After a week in the woods or wherever, it will make more sense."

—Pete Wakeman

Steps to Create a Workable Schedule

- Create to-do lists with time estimates.
- Schedule important work or activities that need creativity and intelligence during your peak energy period.
- Don't book every minute. Leave time to deal with crises and the unexpected.
- Combine tasks; for example, open mail while you boot up your computer.
- Determine what time you want to finish work and leave the office. Then proceed backward, putting the most important tasks in your schedule first.
- Identify tasks to work on when you have unexpected free time.
- Keep your schedule easily accessible. Check on your progress throughout the day to see if you are on target.
- Share your schedule with others to reinforce your attention to time management.
- Record your progress.
- Congratulate yourself every time you hit a target!

Delegate creatively

Once you've determined areas where you want to reduce time, be creative about how you delegate. Look for opportunities wherever you find them. Vendors such as financial institutions may provide services that save you time.

"The admin is incredibly busy, just like you are. There's only so much you can put on her plate. So when I got a direct-mail piece from a credit-card company offering automated itemized expense reports, I looked into it. I am working with my company to integrate this service into our expense management process, which will save time for a lot of people since many of us use the same card."

—Beth Chapman

Delegate for results

When you delegate, focus on the results, not the process. People approach problems in different ways, so remain open to the variety of potential solutions.

With that in mind, try the following:

- Identify tasks to delegate. In addition to tasks that do not contribute to key activities, consider jobs that other people do better than you can.

- Keep in mind that a job you dislike might be an interesting challenge for someone else. You may hate checking everyone's expense reports. Someone else might not mind a detailed-oriented task.

- Identify the right person for the job. Consider his time, personality, and skill. Even if someone can't do the job as well as you do, a job-training session may be all that is needed to help.

- Communicate expectations clearly, including the requirements for success, time line, and budget. Work together so you both understand what success means. Share relevant information, such as previous research and best practices. Introduce the key people who are involved.

- Delegate authority along with responsibility. Anyone attempting to do a job without proper authority will become frustrated and ineffective.

- Let go. Don't micromanage. Give people the room they need to do the job in their own way.

How to Overcome Obstacles

I t takes practice, persistence, and self-awareness to apply the principles of time leveraging and management in your everyday life. As you begin to work toward your goals and adjust your schedule, you'll encounter obstacles that prevent you from using your time effectively. Part of leveraging your time means recognizing these obstacles and working to overcome them.

Recognize common obstacles to managing your time

What sorts of problems are preventing you from leveraging your time? Here are some common difficulties many people have to cope with:

- a chaotic, noisy, demanding working environment

- a poorly organized work space

- a tendency to procrastinate and put off work that needs to be done now

- inefficient meetings and unnecessary travel.

Recognizing the problem is the first step in solving it. Don't feel overwhelmed. Tackle one obstacle at a time. Break it down and keep working on it.

Deal with adverse cultures and working environments

The principles of time leveraging can be adapted to even the most interruption-driven and time-sensitive environments. Through experimentation, sensitivity, and determination, managers in these cultures can learn to leverage their time.

Leverage time in an interruption-driven culture. In many companies, the culture is built on open communications, ongoing teamwork, and a sense of constant, synergistic energy. These environments can be exciting, but they can also be highly distracting. Even if you block out time, there's no guarantee that someone won't pop in or a problem won't suddenly arise. While interruptions can be difficult, managers in cultures like these are expected to be available.

For example, Michael Rothman, a software developer who often works as the tech lead on product releases, has developed several ways to manage his time and be an effective manager.

"Having an open door is a very high priority in the culture of the kinds of companies I work for. You can close your door and people take that as a sign that now is not a good time, but you can't do it a lot."
—Michael Rothman

Another way Michael handles interruptions is to use them to accomplish several things at once. Michael relies heavily on a personal digital assistant (PDA), which he refers to at least 12 times a day. The PDA contains to-do lists for every project he's working on.

What Would YOU Do?

Knock, Knock, Who's There?

Paul wearily turned to his spreadsheets when Carol left. He really hadn't meant to spend the last half hour talking about the company's dental insurance plan, but he was committed to his open-door policy. And it was working. Morale was up. Roland, Paul's predecessor, had been so inaccessible that you'd have to make an appointment with him to tell him that the building was burning down. What a relief it was when Roland was promoted to vice president.

But Paul's accessibility had its drawbacks. He spent all day talking to people, and all night doing the work he should have been doing during the day. He couldn't keep running this chat room. He was becoming exhausted. How could he remain available to his employees and get his work done too?

What would YOU do? See *What you COULD do*.

> **Tip:** Progress, not perfection. Your goal isn't
> perfection; your goal is improvement. Every time
> you get a little better at managing your time,
> you move closer to one of your goals.

"I try to synchronize the interrupts. So if someone comes to see me, I determine if what they're talking about is something I can or need to do right away. If it isn't, I can put it on the list. And while the person is in the office, I can pull up the list and go over several things that the two of us might need to talk about, so the interruption becomes a lot more useful."
—Michael Rothman

Michael minimizes interruptions by scheduling regular meetings.

"I have regular meetings, and I really encourage people to defer any-thing super-important to the regular meeting [if possible], *which makes the meeting useful. What I want is for them to collect things that come up all week for the meeting, unless it's something that has to be resolved right away."*
—Michael Rothman

Michael wasn't always as well organized as he is now. It took a process of trial and error—and the purchase of a PDA—before he began to work as effectively as he does now.

> **Tip:** Review the types of interruptions that tend to occur, and try to develop contingency plans. Then authorize others to deal with the problems if they happen again.

"Most of the time I'm the manager or tech lead, and the nature of the work is very interrupt-driven. I'd usually have eight things I was working on and I'd lose track, and it was frustrating. I'd be working furiously on project C and D for a couple of days, and forget entirely about project A. So I experimented. I had paper lists and other strategies. When I got the PDA, I threw it all away. I have one list. Now, anytime anything occurs to me, anything I have to do, I just add to it on my PDA."

—Michael Rothman

Another advantage of a planning and organizing tool such as the PDA is in helping Michael to manage up.

"One of the nice things about the computer is you now have a list of all the things you did. So on a weekly basis I use that list in a meeting with my manager. If it's something that got checked off the list, it's saved. If you're working on something, it's starred. So at the end of the week, the progress report is already done."

—Michael Rothman

Handle interruptions effectively. You can often delegate the handling of interruptions. But in the cases where you are the only one who can address the interruption, deal with it quickly, so you can return to your priority tasks. Even when handling an interruption takes half the day, focus your energy on the time in the day you have left.

You do not always need to be open for visitors. In some cases, you may find it appropriate to refuse to see a visitor without an appointment.

For example,

- Determine whether your unexpected visitor has an immediate crisis or an issue that has to be dealt with quickly.

- Schedule another time to meet with the visitor, if possible. (You can say, *"I think I can help you, but right now I'm in the middle of something. Can we meet after lunch about this?"*)

- Refer the visitor to another appropriate person, if possible. (You can say, *"I can't pull away right now, but check with Bob and see if he can help. Let me know what the two of you work out."*)

- Make a note of where you are before you break away from your work, and return to that task after the interruption.

If necessary, accept the interruption, take follow-up action, and then recapture your mental position before the interruption. But that's not always easy to do.

Leverage your time in a time-sensitive business

Some businesses are extremely time-sensitive. You must work in the moment almost all day, dealing with customers, answering phones, solving problems. But even in industries such as food services, hospitality, health care, and financial services you can leverage time and move toward concrete goals.

As an equity analyst who follows the stock market during the day, Elisabeth Choi has to synthesize a constant flow of information, opinions, ideas, and news, but, at the same time, she must research stocks and look for opportunities down the road.

"You're looking for bits and pieces of information. All of a sudden, pieces fall into place and you have a picture, but not all the pieces are there. But enough of a picture emerges so you can say 'aha.' It's called the mosaic theory. You're never operating with everything, but you're trying to get enough pieces to reach a conviction. The notes you take when you have conversations, everything you read, all that information that goes into forming the mosaic. By managing your time well, you get more pieces of the mosaic to fall into place."
—Elisabeth Choi

Due to the nature of the stock market, Elisabeth doesn't create a tight weekly work schedule. Instead, she has developed strategies that allow her to snatch chunks of useful time as they pop up. She creates a separate computer file for each stock she is covering. In each file, she enters key information and questions, as well as notes she takes during all the conversations she has about the stock. She is always prepared to leverage the brief, unpredictable time she has with hard-to-reach analysts and company representatives. Each file is a valuable and quick-access reference tool because she can find important details and questions when she needs them.

"These people are very, very busy and they have a lot of competing demands on their time. So you have to be organized and ready to ask questions. You have to be really, really good about taking notes. When I work on a stock, I come up with a list and write out questions about what information I want. Three or four days might go by, and the analyst finally calls back at 2:00 p.m. on Friday afternoon. You quickly pull up your notes or pull up your e-mail. You have the questions right there. And you take down everything you talk about in that conversation, because you're not going to remember it next week or next month. Say you talk to a CFO this quarter; well, you can go back to your notes and then say to him later, 'You said this last quarter; how is it going this quarter?'"

—Elisabeth Choi

A high-pressure, time-sensitive environment can make it difficult to set aside any time at all, let alone time to work on long-range goals. For Elisabeth, organization, note-taking, and discipline allow her to look for chunks of time so she can work on longer-term research.

*"When the market's slow, I can take a couple of hours to study a stock I want to decide on in two weeks. And if I have to stop, I take a minute to ask, 'At this point, where does my opinion stand, what is the pic-*ture? What are the three things I still don't know enough about to make an informed decision? Do I want to know more about their customer diversification? What does their balance sheet look like? Their inventory?' *I'll make a note in the file that those are the three*

things I want to look at, so when I open up the file next time I know where I left off, and I remember my thought process."

—Elisabeth Choi

Elisabeth's organization saves her valuable time, as well as the time of the busy people she communicates with during the day.

"E-mail has really helped me a lot because I send a list of questions or issues I want to talk about to the company contact or the analyst. If I can't reach them on the phone right away, I can prepare them for the conversation I want to have. I send a quick e-mail about the four things I want to discuss, so they can either respond by e-mail or we can set up a time when I know they'll be there. E-mail helps everyone make the best use of time because we both know what we're going to talk about, and we don't waste time playing phone tag."

—Elisabeth Choi

Deal with disorganized work spaces

For many people, a lack of organization stymies their efforts to use time effectively. There's nothing rewarding about pawing through papers, mail, files, and receipts that are piled up all over every work surface. It wastes time and it's frustrating. Fortunately, there is help for the organizationally impaired (see Office Space Planning Tool on the next page).

> *"Uncluttering your stuff helps you unclutter your mind."*
> —Sandy Block

In her successful business as the Clutter Cutter, Sandy Block helps people organize their work spaces so they can make best use

Category/Item Type	Container and Tips
Bills to be paid	Plastic drawer in a fairly accessible place
Must-do today	An open-top bin. Give yourself easy access in a visible place; empty this bin every day.
Have-to-do soon	A closed-top bin. Monitor this pile carefully to see if it needs subdivision.
To file	Open-top bin. File completed items such as signed contracts, tax documents, and so on that you need once or twice a year or that you need for legal purposes.
Reading materials—journals, newsletters, etc.	Store professional publications that you use as reference materials in magazine holders and place on a shelf near or above the desk where they are easily accessible. Recycle the rest.
Magazines	Put periodicals in a bin on a table or public place so others can read them, or put them in a tote bag so you can carry them to read elsewhere.
Price lists and catalogs	Depending on how frequently you refer to these items, use either closed-top bins or magazine holders. When a new issue or list comes, recycle the old one!
Outgoing items	Place a bin in a highly visible area near the door for outgoing packages, regular mail, or any item that needs to be handed off to someone else, such as a contract that must be signed. Empty it by the end of each day.
Papers for projects	Use a large document box or a cardboard file box for each project or client. When the project is no longer active, store the box in case any material is needed later.
Instruction manuals and warranties	Plastic, closed-top containers are made for this purpose. These documents do not usually need to be highly accessible.
Small items, pens, pencils, stickies, paper clips, etc.	All kinds of containers are made for these items. Drawer separators are also handy.
CDs	Put CDs into CD binders and then store them like books, or use metal mesh CD boxes.

of their time. Sandy has loved to organize space since she was seven years old.

"I grew up in a very messy house and one day a friend walked in and couldn't believe how messy it was, and I was so embarrassed I was sent into a spin, and I've been organizing ever since. In fifth

grade, when I was house-sitting for a neighbor, I organized every room. Just recently, we stayed at [my husband's] cousin's house. I kept looking for the salt, and it was always in a different place, so I completely reorganized the kitchen. I couldn't stand it. I enjoy doing it, but my kids will probably grow up to be messy because I make them be so orderly."

—Sandy Block, the Clutter Cutter

Over the years, Sandy has developed an easy-to-follow system for helping people get organized, and stay that way.

"The biggest problem people have is feeling overwhelmed. They don't feel they have the time to take four hours to organize. No one does that except for people who do it for a living. So don't think you need a four-hour block to get through the process. The first thing you do is realize that you need a place for everything that comes into your office. From there, you can break the whole thing down."

—Sandy Block

"I put serious thought into how to organize the files on my laptop. For example, each client has a file and within each file there are separate folders—such as proposals, deliverables, notes, etc. If I don't need a hard copy (that is, a paper file), I throw it out. Knowing exactly where everything is and eliminating piles of paper has made my life a lot easier. One of my clients, a CEO, noticed what I was doing and has adapted the same technique for himself. We laugh as we carry our laptops around the office, but it really helps."

—Melissa Raffoni,
    Managing Director of Professional Skills

Sandy Block's Seven Steps to Organizing Your Office

1. **Plan.** You need a place for everything that comes into your office. Spend 10 or 20 minutes coming up with a storage plan. What kinds of paperwork do you have? What kinds of bins and storage containers can you put these items in? List the kinds things you need to store and decide where you are going to put them. (Time: 10–30 minutes)

2. **Clear off your desk completely.** (Have a recycle bin, trash can, and/or trash bag handy.) Take everything off your desk and out of your drawers and make one big pile. Clean the desk. This should feel very satisfying. It doesn't matter that everything you have is in a pile now. It's just as inaccessible as it was when it was that big pile on your desk. (Time: 20 minutes)

3. **Do a first-pass throw away.** As you clean off your desk, get rid of as much as you can. You'll save time by having less stuff to store later. Don't get bogged down. Throw away only those things you know you don't want. If you have to think about, just put it in the pile. (Time: 5 minutes)

4. **Shop.** Make a shopping list and remember, there are bins made for just about everything. Go to an office-supply store for most or all of what you need. Art-supply stores also have attractive document boxes as well as containers for pencils, CDs, and other supplies. (Time: 1–2 hours)

5. **Sort.** Put the most obvious items and the things you need immediately into the assigned bins. Put items you use every day in

(continued)

nearby, easy-to-access locations. Be flexible, and remember, you can move things around later. Keep throwing things away as you go. Once you've made a first pass, you'll still have a pile, but your desk will actually be in working order. (Time: 20–40 minutes)

6. Fine-tune your sorting. Pull and sort items from the pile. Now that you have your storage plan, most of the things that you pull from the pile will have a place to go. Throw them out, or put them in their appropriate place or determine a new place. Spend five minutes here and there reducing the pile. (Time: 5–20 minutes)

7. Adjust. At the end of the week, your office may not be perfect, but it is a lot better than it was before. You've made progress. You may find that your to-do box isn't conveniently located or it's too full, but at least you have a to-do box. Keep adjusting according to your priorities. You may need to merge two categories into one, or subdivide a big category into two. Now you have a system, and it's easier to change just one bin than to have to redo the whole pile again. (Time: ongoing, 10–20 minutes as needed)

> **Tip:** Keep receipts, and leave the factory labels and price tags on for the first couple of weeks. That way, if you find you don't like a particular type of bin, you can return it. Label the storage bins with stickies at first. When you're sure a container is working for you, label it in a permanent way.

Confront procrastination

There's an old joke about the sign taped to the door of the room where the Procrastinator's Support Group meets: *"Meeting rescheduled, come back tomorrow."* It's natural to want to avoid unpleasant work, but the putting-off-until-tomorrow syndrome can present itself in subtle guises—so subtle you may not even realize that you are procrastinating. Some common symptoms of procrastination, along with some suggested solutions, are shown on the following page.

If these solutions don't work, and you must perform the task, do whatever is necessary to get through it, but promise yourself you will do whatever you can to prevent the same circumstances from occurring again. Then follow through.

Avoid poorly planned meetings and unnecessary travel

Everyone has faced the frustration of sitting through a poorly planned meeting or has spent time on the road when it wasn't

PROCRASTINATION SYMPTOM	POSSIBLE SOLUTION
Perfectionism	**Let It Go**
Do you ever find it difficult to complete tasks because you want everything to be *"just right"*? Do you keep redoing things or frequently go *"back to the drawing board"*?	• Learn to recognize that your time is as important, if not more so, than perfection. • Maintain a balanced perspective. Get regular reality checks from coworkers by asking if something is ready to sign off on. Then, when you do sign off, let it go! • Realize your tendency to obsess, and stop yourself. Ask yourself, *"Is this really going to make a difference? Is it worth my effort?"*
Overplanning	**Teamwork**
Do you ever prolong the planning process to avoid beginning work? If you must plan for every contingency, you may find yourself going over budget or throwing off your schedule completely.	Overplanning may indicate that you feel overwhelmed. Work with colleagues and coworkers to tackle the problem and get started. The efforts and perspective of even one other person can often overcome this type of procrastination. Don't be afraid to ask others to help.
Deadline High	**Tighter Scheduling**
Do you ever delay work because you find it stimulating to work against a tight deadline?	An individual contributor may be able to carry off this style effectively, but if you're on a team, this behavior can frustrate other team members, and you may compromise the quality of the job due to lack of time. Work hard to create a schedule and stick to it—especially if others are relying on your contributions or leadership.
Comfort Tasks	**Guidance**
Do you ever revert to tasks you *used* to enjoy and are good at, in order to put off more challenging work?	• You may be avoiding tasks because you are unsure about how to proceed. • Don't be afraid to ask for help from someone who has the skills. Seek advice from a supervisor or a coworker if a task seems too difficult. • Analyze the skills needed to complete the task.
You Don't Want to Do It	**Creativity**
Nothing subtle about this one. You know you are putting it off, and you know why: you don't want to do it.	• Delegate the task to someone who *does* want to do it. • If delegating doesn't work, set an arbitrary start and go from there. • Create a reward for when you finish. For example, if you dread writing a report but you enjoy returning phone calls, write the report first and return the phone calls when the report is finished.

necessary. You may not always be able to control these situations, but there are some ways to improve them.

Make meetings productive for you. A few simple strategies can help you maximize the time you spend in meetings.

- Before you attend any meeting, decide whether you are the best representative. If you do decide it's worth your time, make sure that the meeting has clear objectives and proposed outcomes.

- If you have not received an agenda for the meeting, request to see it in advance. Let others know you cannot send the best person until you know more about the purpose of the meeting.

- Arrange to attend only the part of the meeting that is relevant to you.

- If you are running the meeting, send out the agenda and points to consider before the meeting. This ensures that you maximize all the participants' time and keep the meeting on track. If possible, ask the participants to prepare in advance to improve the effectiveness of the meeting.

⁇hat You COULD Do.

Let's go back to Paul's problem.

Paul needs to meet with each of his employees individually and explain his dilemma. He can make it clear that being accessible is critical to him, but he needs to find a way to get some work done. He should also explain that he would like to learn more about them and how they can more effectively work together so he can help and guide them appropriately. Employees will appreciate the candidness as well as the personal interest Paul is taking in customizing his approach to managing each of them.

He can ask open-ended questions such as:

- What direction, information, or feedback do you need from me to better do your job?
- What do you like or not like about my management style? What could I do differently?
- How would you prefer that we communicate—scheduled meetings? Lunch? Stopping in as needed? E-mail?
- How often and for how long should I expect to meet with you on a regular basis?

After these one-on-one discussions, Paul can make a game plan with each employee. Depending on each one's response, Paul most likely will end up trying for a balance of scheduled and open-door interactions.

Regarding the open-door policy, Paul needs to explore manageable ways to deal with the interruptions and ask the following to get input:

- Is there a certain part of the day when he is more needed than others?
- Can he expect some of the current interruptions to wait until the scheduled meetings?
- How would the direct report feel if Paul closed the door to his office, grabbed a conference room, or came in to the office later if he needed quiet time?
- What is a reasonable amount of quiet time that he should expect to have in a given day?

Now that Paul has communicated the issue to his employees, has a better sense of their individual needs, and has received their input, he can make better decisions about how to manage his time.

Minimize business travel. If you are asked to travel for business, find out if it is necessary to hold the meetings face-to-face rather than via conference call. If the trip is necessary, make sure that you are the best person to make the trip. If not, arrange to have the right person travel instead of you.

When you do have to travel, try to make waiting and in-transit time as productive as possible.

- Organize your materials before the trip, reviewing all background information you may need on the road.

- Take a well-organized briefcase with you.

- Use cell phones and laptops.

- Bring a pile of work or reading or a list of phone calls to make en route.

Take time to avoid or overcome obstacles

All of the problems discussed above can be dealt with by taking the time to do so. Thus, to leverage your time you have to use time. The process doesn't magically occur—it takes a commitment of your time, planning, and resources, but it is time well spent!

How to Develop Good Time-Management Habits

The big picture helps you determine what your goals are and how to move closer to them. Tools such as time-boxing provide resources for putting your use of time into perspective and creating a proactive method for you to leverage your time the way you want to. There are also many simple habits you can develop to maximize your time usage as well.

Manage messages

Most messages today come via the telephone, e-mail, or fax machine. Here are some ways to manage the often disrupting (and occasionally overwhelming) flow of messages.

Develop effective telephone manners. For many, phone calls are a constant interruption. To make the best use of phone time:

- Screen calls using caller ID or voice mail.

- Refer the caller to someone else if possible.

- Keep the call brief and focused.

- Carve out a block of time in the day when you take phone calls and return them.

- When you really need to focus, take work to a room without a phone.

- Use e-mail to accomplish as much communication as possible.

> **Tip:** Handle paper once. Respond
> to it, file it, pass it along, or toss it out.

Steps for Taking Phone Notes

1. Use your computer and your telephone simultaneously. If you often write while talking on the phone, get a headset to plug into the side of the phone. They're not expensive and help prevent neck strain.

2. On your computer, create a separate file for each account, project, or similar category.

3. Before a conversation, list questions you need to ask and information you want to share.

4. Enter the time, date, and people involved in conversation.

5. Write (or enter) the conversation's purpose.

6. List key information received.

7. List follow-up items you and others need to deal with.

8. List items still outstanding.

9. Use logical naming conventions so you can easily access the information within the proper computer folders; for example, a call made to Acme Tech on April 30, 2005 could be coded as 043005Acme_Weekly call.

Use e-mail to save time. E-mail can be just as disruptive as the telephone if you feel the need to open and respond to every message as it comes in. E-mail can be one of the great time-savers of business today if it's managed wisely. The most important e-mail rule is to keep your messages short and simple.

Here are some other ways to make e-mail work for you:

- Ask short, easy-to-answer questions, for example, *"What is the date of your arrival?" "I'd like to contact the caterer you used for your luncheon. Please send the name and number."*

- Keep colleagues, customers, or suppliers updated on ongoing progress. For example, write *"We sent the samples you requested by overnight on Thursday at 4:00. They should arrive Friday before 10:00."*

- E-mail is not a substitute for human interaction. *Do not* use e-mail for messages that may have emotional impact, especially if it's negative, such as, *"I am disappointed in the quality of your report" or "I am sorry to inform you that you are being laid off."*

- Alert others to changes that can save time. For instance, write, *"Our 3:00 meeting has been moved from the Fishbowl into Conference Room B."*

- Group several questions together and number them so the recipient can easily copy and reply, answering several items at once.

- Avoid time-wasting missed telephone calls by setting up call dates on e-mail.

- Save e-mails into relevant project files for quick reference later.

Be an efficient e-mailer. Are you an efficient e-mailer? Do you . . .

- use key words in subject lines to give the recipient a clue about the e-mail's content?

- always include your phone number so recipients can get back to you by telephone? (Most e-mail programs have a set-signature function that lets you set up a standard signature.)

- edit your e-mails for brevity and "skim-ability" so the reader can quickly scan the e-mail and take away your main points? Break up text by formatting with white space, headers, and bullet points (such as used here)?

- try to make the e-mail fit into one screen field so the reader does not have to scroll down?

Tip: Straighten up each evening before you leave. It will help you start the next day with a clear mind.

TASKS TO FILL DOWN TIME

5-Minute Blocks	10-Minute Blocks	30-Minute Blocks
Schedule an appointment.	Make a brief phone call.	Skim journals, magazines, newspapers.
Write a quick note.	Outline an agenda for a meeting.	Plan your weekly schedule.
Update your schedule.	Read and respond to e-mail.	Outline notes for a report.
	Plan an upcoming trip.	Fill out an expense report.

Take advantage of unexpected down time. This down time often occurs when you're traveling or when meetings start late. Since this is time that usually can't be used in the pursuit of a meaningful personal goal, use it to be more productive.

Tip: Sort mail while you are going from the mailroom to the office. Toss out junk mail before you even sit down. Immediately sort the rest of the mail into categories, such as "*to-be-paid*" or "*to-do today.*"

Tools and Resources

Tools and Resources for Shaping Your Career

Discovery Log

This easy exercise can yield surprisingly insightful results and help you to keep a running list of what you observe or experience about a job or work environment that you like—or don't like. The list items could be about your job or others' and about tasks, relationships, or the environment itself. They could range from "I need to work near a window" to "I can't stand working alone for long periods of time." Since this log is for your eyes only, be blunt and don't censor. After a period of time, review the list to see what themes emerge. Decide what the items tell you about your core business interests and work reward values that can be useful in managing your career.

What I Like	What I Dislike

Skills Assessment

Use this form to develop a baseline assessment of your skills, including those that are transferable from one position to another or those that you want to develop. Rate your current level of proficiency, if desired, from 1 (low, beginning level) to 5 (high, expert level). You may want to supplement this form with skills assessment tools that relate directly to your position, which may be available from your company. You can also use this form to solicit peer feedback on your skill level. Obviously, some of the skills listed below will have no bearing on your career, present or future. Feel free to pass on any such items.

Date of Assessment:

Skill	Level of Proficiency Low 1 2 3 4 5 High					Transferable Yes	No	Key Skill I Want to Develop
Communication Skills								
Writing About Business								
Writing Proposals								
Making Presentations								
Facilitating								
Running Meetings								
Listening								
Interviewing								
Influencing								
Giving and Receiving Feedback								
Resolving Conflicts								
Negotiating								
Writing Creative or Promotional Materials								
Communicating by E-mail								
Editing								
Proofreading								
Writing Job Descriptions								
Other:								
Technology and Computer Skills								
Keyboarding								
Word Processing								
Using Spreadsheets								
Working with HTML								
Working with XML								
Managing Projects								
Using E-mail								
Using Presentation Software								
Using Graphics Software								
Other:								

continued

Skill	Level of Proficiency Low 1 2 3 4 5 High		Transferable Yes	No	Key Skill I Want to Develop
Financial Skills					
Budgeting					
Analyzing Financial Information					
Cost Accounting					
Forecasting					
Tracking and Managing					
Preparing a Business Plan					
Preparing an Investment Initiative					
Analyzing Cash Flow					
Determining Breakeven Point					
Using Quantitative Analysis					
Other:					
Supervisory Skills					
Hiring					
Coaching					
Delegating					
Setting Goals and Objectives					
Directing					
Assessing Performance					
Leading					
Motivating					
Training					
Analyzing Work Flow and Processes					
Recruiting and Retaining Employees					
Managing Administrative Tasks					
Other:					
Management Skills					
Leading Change					
Managing Customers, Internal and/or External					
Orchestrating Projects					
Managing Production or Implementation					
Managing Your Boss					
Solving Business Problems					
Thinking Critically About Business Issues					
Consulting and Networking					
Managing Vendors					
Planning Strategy					
Planning Tactics					
Thinking Creatively, Brainstorming					
Managing for Innovation					
Managing a Diverse Workforce					
Marketing for International Sales					
Teamwork Skills					
Leading a Team					
Engaging in Group Problem Solving					

Skill	Level of Proficiency Low 1 2 3 4 5 High		Transferable Yes	No	Key Skill I Want to Develop
Teamwork Skills, *continued*					
Keeping Teams on Target					
Working with a Virtual Team					
Assuming Team Membership Roles					
Collaborating					
Other:					
Self-Management Skills					
Knowing Yourself					
Cultivating Emotional Intelligence					
Managing Your Time					
Balancing Work and Life					
Developing Your Career					
Handling Stress					
Setting Limits and Goals					
Using Power and Authority Positively					
Seeing Multiple Perspectives					
Other:					
Sales and Marketing Skills					
Marketing Products or Services					
Engaging in Direct Marketing					
Performing or Directing Market Research					
Telemarketing					
Developing Promotions					
Handling Publicity					
Using Electronic Marketing					
Managing Trade Shows/Exhibits					
Marketing to Consumers					
Marketing to Businesses					
Analyzing the Competition					
Engaging in Direct Sales					
Forecasting Sales					
Engaging in Telesales					
Engaging Consultative Selling					
Other:					
Physical and Manual Dexterity Skills					
Assembling, Constructing, or Building					
Operating Tools or Machinery					
Fixing or Repairing					
Training Others on Tasks					
Other Industry and/or Job-Specific Skills (List)					

Informational Interviewing

Use this form to help you prepare for an informational interview.

Discussion with: **Date:**

Objectives

What do you really want to get out of this interview? What would make it successful for you?

Marketplace

What are your projections for this type of work or industry? Is it stable, growing, declining?

What are the key trends or issues? New developments? Key challenges?

What and where are the opportunities?

What are typical salaries in this type of job, entry-level to experienced? What are the opportunities for career growth?

Entry into Position

When and how did you get involved in this work?

What was your training and background? Is this typical for people in your position and in similar positions?

How important are specific credentials for entry or success?

Job Specifics

What's a typical day like for you or someone in a similar position?

What do you like most about your work?

What do you like least?

What talents or skills do you think are the most crucial to success in this work?

What attitudes or values are important?

Who doesn't do well in this type of work?

How do you advance or get promoted in this type of work?

Recommendations

Would my background be appropriate for this type of work?

What would you recommend I do if I want to go into this type of work?

Are there other jobs similar to yours that you would suggest I also consider?

Can you recommend other people I can talk to, or other resources I can check out?

Knowing what you do now, would you approach this career (or job) in the same way? If not, what would you do differently, and why?

Rewards

Use this worksheet to think through what really motivates you at work. You can also rate each item from low (1) priority or value to high (5). Review these ratings as you assess your degree of satisfaction with your current job, or use them as a guide to what you'd be looking for in your next position. If you are a supervisor, you may use this as part of a development discussion with a direct report.

	Level of Importance or Value
	Low 1 2 3 4 High 5
Financial Gain This position provides an excellent opportunity for financial reward.	
Power and Influence The position offers the opportunity to exercise power and influence and the chance to be an influential decision maker.	
Lifestyle The position fits with my desired lifestyle. It lets me balance work and life demands and interests.	
Autonomy The position offers me autonomy and independence—the ability to work without a lot of close supervision.	
Affiliation The position lets me work with colleagues I enjoy and admire and gives me a sense of belonging to a group.	
Workspace The location and physical workspace are desirable and offer me benefits such as a pleasing environment, an easy commute, or accessibility to day care.	
Intellectual Stimulation The position is interesting and challenging and offers learning and development opportunities.	
Competence This position offers me the opportunity to build competence or expertise in an area.	
Recognition and Support In this position and work environment, my contributions are recognized and valued. My development is supported as well.	
Other List additional specific rewards that you value.	

Assessment
Reviewing your ratings above, what jumps out at you as most important? Least important? How well does your current job meet your reward needs?

Are there some actions you can take so that your work better satisfies your needs, such as modifying your work, taking on a "stretch" assignment, or spending more time with colleagues you enjoy?

Career Self-Assessment

Use the following questions to help you think through your developmental needs and goals. Supplement this form with others such as the Rewards Worksheet to pull together a plan for your next developmental step.

Current and Future Work Situation

What's the overall fit between your current position and your interests, values, and skills?

What is your overall level of satisfaction with your current position? Are you beginning to sense it's time for a change?

Do you anticipate that any of the following changes will occur in the foreseeable future? (Check all that apply.)

☐ Change in supervisor
☐ Relocation: another part of country or international
☐ Corporate downsizing or merger
☐ Change in the type of work you do
☐ Transfer to another division or part of the company
☐ Change to supervisory role

☐ Change in job
☐ Change in workspace
☐ Change in employer
☐ Promotion
☐ Job redefined or enlarged

What are the implications of any anticipated changes? Will you need to learn new skills? Will a change result in a more or less favorable position for you in terms of job fit and opportunity?

Skills: Strengths and Gaps

What are your top five skills (i.e., those where you have the most proficiency and/or those you enjoy using the most)?

What are the top two or three skills you need to learn in order to grow in your job, advance to the next level, or seek a new job?

What are your key transferable skills—those skills that are not just job-specific but that can be applied to work in many positions? Example: basic computer skills, negotiation skills, financial analysis.

continued

What do you think others would say are your strengths?

The Next Step and Opportunity

As a next step towards your long-term career goals, where do you see yourself six to twelve months from now?

What are some developmental opportunities you can take advantage of?

What parts of your work would you like to continue doing or do with more skill?

What new work activities or positions would you like to try?

What are your short-term career development goals?

What support do you need to achieve them? (Training, people, time, money, etc.)

What do you think others would say about your work and your career aspirations and plans?

Test Yourself

This section offers ten multiple-choice questions to help you identify your baseline knowledge of career management. Answers to the questions are given at the end of the test.

1. What three self-knowledge areas are the most important in defining and navigating your career path?

a. Your five-year goals, family values, and financial needs.

b. Your core business interests, work values, and skills.

c. Your short- and long-term goals, core business interests, and skills.

2. What are the three main information sources for knowing yourself?

a. Yourself, others (colleagues, friends, and family), and assessment tools.

b. Your boss, your nighttime dreams, and a group-therapy program.

c. Your family, your friends, and your career counselor.

3. Who is *most* responsible for management of your career?

  a. Your supervisor.
  b. Your company overall (including its career resources department, if it has one).
  c. You.

4. Of your core business interests, work values, and skills, which one area is the most important in identifying appropriate growth opportunities at work?

  a. Core business interests.
  b. Work values.
  c. Skills.

5. Which of the following is the most important benefit of taking charge of your own career?

  a. You're guaranteed to earn more money and get promoted.
  b. Your company doesn't have to invest in a career center.
  c. You find more satisfaction in your work and become a more valuable employee for your company.

6. Which of the following are examples of the eight core business functions that let you express your deepest work interests?

  a. Enterprise Control, Influence through Language and Ideas, and Using Your Intuition.
  b. Application of Technology, Counseling and Mentoring, and Enterprise Control.
  c. Understanding Spreadsheets, Giving Inspiring Speeches, and Managing Work/Life Balance.

7. Decide whether the following statement is true or false: To better match your work with your core business interests, values, and skills, you can collaborate with your supervisor to redefine your current role.

a. True.
b. False.

8. Which of the following metaphors best captures the nature of career development today as opposed to earlier times?

a. A lattice versus a ladder.
b. A bicycle versus a pogo stick.
c. A moored rowboat versus a ship tossing on the ocean.

9. The best developmental opportunities in your organization:

a. Perfectly match your interests, values, and skills.
b. Stretch you by offering challenges that encourage you to learn new skills and knowledge.
c. Encourage you to try work that you know nothing about.

10. Decide whether the following statement is true or false: To obtain the skills you need to perform in a new position, you must go back to school and earn a degree.

a. True.
b. False.

Answers to test questions

1, b. These three self-knowledge areas together form the basis for guiding and managing your career. By understanding what business activities interest you, what workplace rewards you value most, and what you do best, you can define your professional goals.

2, a. By getting to know your core business interests, work reward values, and skills through self-reflection exercises; by collecting feedback from colleagues, friends, and family; and by using any of the available assessment tools, you compile a powerful body of knowledge that will let you define and pursue the best career opportunities for you.

3, c. The business world has experienced enormous, rapidly accelerating changes. The traditional unspoken contract between employer and employee—in which companies took responsibility for employees' career paths—no longer exists at many companies. Therefore, each of us is responsible for managing our own professional development.

4, a. If you're not passionately interested in your work, you'll soon get bored or burn out—no matter how good you are at your job or how much it offers the rewards you value the most.

5, c. When you manage your own career, you help yourself derive more satisfaction from your work. When you're more satisfied at work, you perform better and feel more committed to your job and organization—which also helps your company.

6, b. All three of these are examples of core business interests. The eight core business interests are (1) Application of Technology, (2) Quantitative Analysis, (3) Theory Development and Conceptual Thinking, (4) Creative Production, (5) Counseling and Mentoring, (6) Managing People and Relationships, (7) Enterprise Control, and (8) Influence through Language and Ideas.

7, a. Always assume that you can redefine your current role to better suit you. If you're a high performer, your supervisor will likely be glad to support your efforts in this area. After all, he or she will get to keep you rather than lose you to another position in the company.

8, a. A lattice conveys the idea that professional development opportunities now exist at all levels and in all departments within most organizations. You can move freely among them depending on which opportunities best suit you and your organization.

9, b. You want development opportunities to help you hone new skills and acquire new knowledge—that's what makes work more satisfying to you, and you more valuable to your company. But don't pick an assignment that stretches you too much. A good rule of thumb is that if you think it will take more than six months to deliver excellent performance in the new role, the assignment probably will be *too* much of a stretch.

10, b. There are many other ways to gain new skills besides going back to school. These include volunteering, reading magazines, sharing jobs, and so forth—steps that don't require the time and expense of getting a new degree.

Frequently Asked Questions

Are core business interests determined when you're young, and do they remain unchanged throughout your life?

They're generally determined by your early twenties. By that time, there's a discernible pattern, and the basic contours of that pattern remain remarkably stable.

How were the eight core business interests developed?

They were developed from analysis of thousands of people's responses on tests about their interests at work. The core interests describe fundamental, essential activities of business work.

What's the most common mistake people make in thinking about their careers?

The most common mistake is basing career decisions on what you think you *should* do or what you *can* do—not on what most interests or moves you. You probably have lots of abilities that you're not interested in applying as a regular part of your work. This is an easy trap to fall into. Another trap, especially for people whose careers are just beginning, is going for the job that pays the most. We each should think at least as much about *learning* as about *earning.*

What are some easy ways for people to identify their core business interests?

You can perform active-imagination exercises, in which you reflect on what kinds of work have most inspired you or captured your attention in the past. You can also flip through six months' worth of issues of *Business Week* or *Fortune* and pay attention to what kinds of articles, advertisements, and so on most draw your attention. Look especially for the difference between feeling that you have to *turn* your attention to a particular topic versus feeling that a topic *pulls* your attention.

Can a person have more than one core business interest?

Yes. Often a person will have two or three main interests, with perhaps one of them most dominant.

How have attitudes toward work and career changed?

There's been a change in the idea of what a job is. Many people don't even use the word *job* anymore; instead, they use *work opportunity.* More and more, there aren't jobs per se, as in, "Here's your job, your title, and your desk, and you'll probably be here for five years." Now you're more likely to hear, "We've got a problem or a project, you've got a skill set and a background that can help us. When it's done, we'll have a conversation, and maybe there will be other problems you can help us with. And maybe there won't." The duration of the work opportunity is therefore the *project* duration.

This is true not just for freelancers but also for full-time employees. You may remain an employee for a long time, but your responsibilities may change regularly. This is also true for employees of *any* age—not just 25-year-olds.

What proportion of people find satisfying work?

It's an ongoing search for everyone these days. People do find it, but we all have to keep refining our concept of it and moving toward it. Even though our core business interests remain stable over time, the opportunities to express them depend on economic and other situations that are constantly changing. So, you've got to frequently reengage with the change process.

How can people broach the subject of career change with their immediate supervisors if their supervisors don't want to lose them?

The best way is to frame the discussion in terms of job sculpting: how you can redefine your current role so that it better matches your core business interests, work reward values, and skills. Also, come prepared with solutions for handling the ramifications of any change. For example, if you want to let go of certain responsibilities, how do you suggest they would be handled? If there's simply no opportunity to redefine your role, explore other opportunities within the company. In firms that emphasize retention, your supervisor will be rewarded for helping good employees find new opportunities inside the company.

If I contact people to request an informational interview or a networking discussion, won't they think that I'm just trying to use them?

No—not if you're sincere and you respect their time. Be sure to show them that you appreciate the information they're sharing. Remember: You're not so much asking for a job as you're asking for information. Most people enjoy talking about their work. Explain that someone else whom the person knows and respects recommended him or her as an excellent person for you to talk with, and ask for just twenty minutes of the person's time.

It seems that required skills are always changing. How can I get the skills I need to keep moving forward in my career?

Many people automatically assume that they have to go back to school to get a degree in order to acquire new skills. That's absolutely not true. Continuing education classes are one less time-consuming and less expensive alternative. But there are lots of other ways to learn, too—such as job shadowing, stretch assignments at work, seminars, video- or audiotapes, books, newsletters, online or distance learning, volunteering opportunities, and so on. The key is to assess your options and pick the best ones for your learning style and your skill needs as well as for your budget and schedule.

Everyone's so busy at my company that no one seems to know what's going on in departments other than their own. How can I find out about work opportunities under these conditions?

You can start talking with people from other departments to find out what kinds of work they do, what the culture is like in those departments, and so forth. Also, try asking to be invited to meetings that you normally might not think of attending. Take advantage of all the companywide events and learning opportunities that your firm offers. That's a great way to simply start getting to know people and learning more about how the company operates. From there, you can begin identifying opportunities and drawing on the network of people you've established for information.

Will my work reward values change much over the years?

They will probably change somewhat, depending on the different phases of life you go through. For example, if you're starting a family, financial security and opportunities for long-term saving might become your top reward value. If you're just starting out in the work world, opportunities to travel might be your most important value.

To Learn More

Articles

Butler, Timothy, and James Waldroop. "Job Sculpting: The Art of Retaining Your Best People." *Harvard Business Review* (February 2000).

> Helping people define their ideal jobs benefits everyone: employees, their managers, and the organization. This article shows how managers can play a central role in this process, retaining valuable employees by customizing work to better match employees' deepest interests.

Butler, Timothy, and James Waldroop. "Understanding 'People People.'" *Harvard Business Review* (June 2004).

> Because people do their best work when it most closely matches their interests, the authors contend, managers can increase productivity by taking into account employees' relational interests and skills when making personnel choices and project assignments. After analyzing the psychological tests of more than 7,000 business professionals, the authors identified four dimensions of relational work: influence, interpersonal facilitation, relational creativity, and team leadership. Understanding these four dimensions will help you get optimal per-

formance from your employees, appropriately reward their work, and assist them in setting career goals. It will also help you make better choices when it comes to your own career development. To get started, try the authors' free online assessment tool, which measures both your orientation toward relational work in general and your interest level in each of its four dimensions.

Gary, Loren. "The Next Ideas: Rethinking Money and Motivation." *Harvard Management Update* (April 2004).

Because our attitudes toward money reveal so much about our personalities, perhaps concerns about money can reveal our deep-seated interests. Ever heard the advice, "Do what you love and the money will follow"? For the last half-century, it's been the prevailing view among management thinkers. But now, social critics and executive coaches alike are struck by the way in which an increasingly affluent culture can make the search for meaning and purpose more difficult and are showing a keen interest in the psychology of money.

Nash, Laura, and Howard Stevenson. "Success That Lasts." *Harvard Business Review* (April 2004).

Nash and Stevenson have built a practical framework for a new way of thinking about success—a way that leads to personal and professional fulfillment instead of feelings of anxiety and stress. The authors' research uncovered four irreducible components of success: happiness (feelings of pleasure or contentment about your life); achievement (accomplishments that compare favorably against similar goals others have strived for); significance (the sense that you've made a positive impact on people you care about); and legacy (a way to establish your values or accomplishments so as to help others find future success). People who achieve lasting success, the authors learned, tend to rely on a kaleidoscope strategy to structure their aspirations and activities. This article explains how to build your own kaleidoscope framework.

Books

Boldt, Laurence G. *Zen and the Art of Making a Living: A Practical Guide to Creative Career Design.* New York: Penguin/Arkana, 1999.

In the author's view, everyone is the "artist" of his or her own life. Part I helps you identify deeply satisfying work. Part II provides practical steps to finding or creating that work. A wealth of worksheets, ideas, and strategies supplement the author's ideas.

Butler, Timothy. *Getting Unstuck: How Dead Ends Become New Paths.* Boston: Harvard Business School Press, 2007.

The author provides strategies for moving beyond a career impasse—by recognizing the state of impasse, awakening your imagination, recognizing patterns of meaning in your life, and taking action for change. Drawing on a wealth of stories about individuals who have successfully transitioned out of impasses, this book gives you a practical, authoritative road map for moving past your immediate impasse—and defining a meaningful path forward.

Butler, Timothy, and James Waldroop. *Discovering Your Career in Business.* Cambridge, MA: Perseus Books, 1997.

This book presents the theoretical framework behind the Harvard ManageMentor PLUS "Managing Your Career" topic and the authors' Internet-based career self-assessment and management program, CareerLeader. The authors provide valuable case examples and exercises for identifying your core business interests.

Butler, Timothy, and James Waldroop. *Maximum Success: Changing the Twelve Behavior Patterns That Keep You from Getting Ahead.* New York: Currency/Doubleday, 2000.

Part of managing your own career development is knowing which behaviors are keeping you from your full potential. Using nearly forty years of field research, the authors describe the twelve most common problem-behavior patterns, explore the psychological reasons behind them, and show you how to change them for maximum performance.

Wademan, Daisy. *Remember Who You Are: Life Stories That Inspire the Heart and Mind.* Boston: Harvard Business School Press, 2004.

Leadership requires many attributes besides intelligence and business savvy—courage, character, compassion, and respect are just a few. New managers learn concrete skills in the classroom or on the job, but where do they hone the equally important human values that will guide them through a career that is both successful and meaningful? In this inspirational book, the author gathers lessons on balancing the personal and professional responsibilities of leadership from faculty members of Harvard Business School. Offering a rare glimpse inside the classrooms in which many of the world's prominent leaders are trained, *Remember Who You Are* imparts lessons learned not in business but in life.

Sources

We would like to acknowledge the sources who aided in developing this topic.

Billington, Jim. "Meet Your New Mentor: It's a Network." *Harvard Management Update* (August 1997).

Boldt, Laurence G. *Zen and the Art of Making a Living: A Practical Guide to Creative Career Design.* New York: Penguin/Arkana, 1999.

Bolles, Richard N. *The Three Boxes of Life and How to Get Out of Them.* Berkeley, CA: Ten Speed Press, 1981.

Butler, Timothy, and James Waldroop. *Discovering Your Career in Business.* Cambridge, MA: Perseus Books, 1997.

———. "Job Sculpting: The Art of Retaining Your Best People." *Harvard Business Review* (September–October 1999).

Carlone, Katie. Personal communication. September 13, 2000.

Farren, Caela. *Who's Running Your Career?* Austin, TX: Bard Press, 1997.

Hakim, Cliff. *We Are All Self-Employed.* San Francisco: Berrett-Koehler, 1994.

Hill, Linda. "Managing Your Career." Harvard Business School Note, December 15, 1998. Product no. 9-494-082.

Koonce, Richard. "How to Prevent Professional Obsolescence." *Training & Development* (February 1999).

McCall, Jr., Morgan W. *High Flyers: Developing the Next Generation of Leaders.* Boston: Harvard Business School Press, 1998.

Moses, Barbara. *The Good News about Careers: How You'll Be Working in the Next Decade.* San Francisco: Jossey-Bass, 1999.

Waterman, Jr., Robert H., Judith A. Waterman, and Betsy A. Collard. "Toward a Career-Resilient Workforce." *Harvard Business Review* (July–August 1994).

Tools and Resources for Managing Stress

Life Changes as Stressors Checklist

Change, even positive change, involves stress. Listed below are some common stressful events. Check off the ones that apply to you, and add them up to get a picture of your current stress level and some of its sources. Use this information to select strategies that can help you manage or diminish your stress level.

Personal Changes

- ☐ Personal injury/illness/handicap
- ☐ Pregnancy (your or partner's)
- ☐ End of a relationship
- ☐ Life changes (such as a certain birthday, menopause)
- ☐ Change in self-worth

- ☐ Change in financial status
- ☐ Sexual concerns or difficulties
- ☐ Decision to quit smoking or other substance use
- ☐ Decision to diet
- ☐ Values conflict

Other:

Family Changes

- ☐ Marriage
- ☐ Family member(s) leaving home
- ☐ New family member(s)
- ☐ Separation/divorce
- ☐ Trouble with in-laws or other family members

- ☐ Partner starting or stopping a job
- ☐ Illness/healing of a family member
- ☐ Death of a close friend or family member
- ☐ Parent/child tensions

Other:

Work Changes

- ☐ Change in workload
- ☐ Change in pay
- ☐ Start of a new job
- ☐ Promotion/demotion
- ☐ Change in relationships at work

- ☐ New supervisor
- ☐ Retirement
- ☐ Change in hours
- ☐ Change in job security/layoff
- ☐ Merger or acquisition

Other:

Environmental Changes

- ☐ Natural disaster (earthquake, fire, flood)
- ☐ War or conflict
- ☐ Move to a new house or apartment
- ☐ Move to a new neighborhood

- ☐ Move to a new city
- ☐ Move to a new climate
- ☐ Move to a new culture or country
- ☐ Remodeling project
- ☐ Crime in neighborhood

Other:

Workplace Stress Assessment

*Use this informal assessment to help identify (either by yourself or with a work group)
the current level of positive and negative stress in your work environment.
Then discuss or brainstorm strategies that can either increase the positive energy
level or diminish the unhealthy dis-stress.*

Positive Stress

I think the current level of **positive, energizing** stress in my (our) workplace is: (Check one.)

☐ low ☐ moderately low ☐ average ☐ moderately high ☐ high

Positive sources of energizing stress include: (Check all that apply.)

☐ Challenging but attainable goals
☐ The ability and resources to meet critical deadlines
☐ Team spirit, a "we-can-do-it" attitude
☐ Diverse or innovative assignments that stretch
   employees

☐ Effective leadership that motivates
☐ Solution of new problems
☐ The opportunity to learn new skills
☐ The resources to deal effectively
   with a crisis

Others:

Ideas I have to increase energizing stress (for example, a friendly competition) are:

Negative Stress

I think the current level of **negative, toxic** stress in my (our) workplace is: (Check one.)

☐ low ☐ moderately low ☐ average ☐ moderately high ☐ high

Negative stress is being shown in: (Check all that apply.)

☐ Increased irritability or temper outbursts
☐ Conflicts between team members
☐ Increased absenteeism or numbers of sick days
☐ Higher levels of errors and mistakes

☐ Overall reduction in productivity
☐ Increase in employee burnout,
   turnover
☐ People "tuning out," decreased
   engagement

Others:

Ideas I have to reduce toxic stress are:

The single action that, if implemented, would make the greatest positive difference is:

Workload

How would you rate your workload (or that of the group)?

☐ Too low   ☐ Just right   ☐ Too high

Is this situation temporary, long-standing, or subject to change?

Is the workload stimulating or overwhelming?

If the workload needs adjustment, are there any work processes (how the work is done) that could be changed, eliminated, or modified? Which ones?

Are there opportunities to change the amount of work by adjusting deadlines, outsourcing, hiring more temporary or permanent help, or taking other measures? Can you rotate assignments? Take some time off? Other ideas to prevent overload or burnout?

Test Yourself

This section offers ten multiple-choice questions to help you identify your baseline knowledge of the essentials of managing stress. Answers to the questions are given at the end of the test.

1. All stress and worry should be avoided. True or false?

   a. True.

   b. False.

2. Some of the most common sources of stress in the workplace are:

   a. Physical illnesses.

   b. Changes in the workplace and an unhealthy work environment.

   c. Concerns about home life's effect on work.

3. The four steps for breaking out of the negative stress cycle are:

   a. Breathe. Reflect. Choose. Act.

   b. Consult friends. Relax. Get a massage. Take a walk.

   c. Stop. Breathe. Reflect. Choose.

4. In what ways can connectedness help reduce stress?

    a. Connecting with solutions can reduce stressful situations.

    b. Connections with trusted people, particularly colleagues, can provide you with reassurance and can help you gain perspective and perhaps new ideas for solutions.

    c. Offices that are technologically connected help reduce the stress of dealing with outdated networks or a lack of networks.

5. Chronic worriers often subject themselves to negative automatic thoughts that contribute to their worry and stress. True or false?

    a. True.

    b. False.

6. Which of the following is the easiest, cheapest, and most natural antidote to worry?

    a. Exercising.

    b. Eating healthfully.

    c. Sleeping restfully.

7. What do you need to prepare for the relaxation response?

    a. A dark room, a bed or cot, and soft music.

    b. A spiritual guide.

    c. A quiet environment, a mental device, a passive attitude, and a comfortable position.

8. Which of the following activities can be used as stress busters?

a. Playing video games.

b. Laughing about an amusing story.

c. Taking a coffee break.

9. Which of the following is *not* an effective response to a colleague who tells you he's extremely worried about something?

a. Use body language to show your concern.

b. Suggest several possible solutions to his problem.

c. Provide occasional verbal acknowledgment.

10. The most effective way to counter the negative effects of toxic worry is to:

a. Reverse the worry equation by increasing your sense of power and decreasing your sense of vulnerability.

b. Solve the problems that are causing the worry.

c. Ensure that you get sufficiently restful sleep.

Answers to test questions

1, b. This statement is actually false. All stress and worry should *not* be avoided. Some stress is actually good because it can provide you with the extra energy you need to deal with situations. To the extent that stress helps you prepare for difficult times, you can benefit from it.

2, b. One common source of stress in the workplace is change in the workplace—whether a positive change (such as a new assignment) or a negative one (such as an increase in workload). Another major source of stress is an unhealthy work environment marked by interpersonal conflicts or confusing expectations.

3, c. These four steps are effective in breaking the negative stress cycle. When you stop, you block the negative messages you're telling yourself. When you breathe, you calm your body. Then you can reflect on the problem and choose the best action to take.

4, b. Connections with trusted people are the most powerful antidote to stress because those individuals can listen to you and help you see a stressful situation in a different light. Remember one of the first rules in taking charge of worry and stress: Never worry alone!

5, a. Chronic worriers tend to make their problems worse by listening to their own negative automatic thoughts instead of looking at the actual situation. To combat chronic worrying, you can reshape such negative self-talk into more positive and healthy messages.

6, a. Exercise helps you break out of the physical immobility that stress often causes. Even brief physical efforts, such as standing up and stretching, can clear your mind of the weight of worry. Exercise reduces tension, eases aggression and frustration, increases your sense of well-being, improves sleep, and aids concentration.

7, c. You don't need much to prepare for the relaxation response. All you really need is a quiet environment where you can focus on relaxing. Then you find a comfortable position, concentrate on a single word or sound, and push away distracting thoughts.

8, b. Humor is a wonderful antidote to stress, and laughter is a natural and healthy way to release tension and put aside serious thoughts for awhile. Try finding the humor in your everyday life—but remember not to confuse genuine humor with ridicule. Humor enriches us all; ridicule hurts us all.

9, b. To listen effectively to a worried colleague, it's best not to try to solve the problem but instead to understand it. If you want to comment, do so only on what your colleague is describing, rather than offering possible solutions to the problem. In addition, use body language to show your concern and provide occasional verbal acknowledgment, such as "I understand" or "I see."

10, a. In any stressful situation, you can reduce the negative effects of toxic worry by increasing your sense of power and control and decreasing your sense of vulnerability. Strategies for increasing power and decreasing vulnerability include structuring your activities, connecting with people who can listen, and taking care of your health. All of these strategies give you the power to better manage your stress.

Frequently Asked Questions

How common are stress-related problems at work?

Extremely common. With heavy workloads, career pressure, and demands for increased productivity in almost all areas of the workplace, stress is a constant factor in our professional lives. Some stress is good—it gets people going—but too much can have the opposite effect. Excessive stress is repetitive and frustrating with no reward and no satisfaction, and it can become toxic, doing real damage to your mind and body.

Don't I have to be stressed to succeed in today's professional environment?

To a degree, yes. Stress does stimulate performance. Some people thrive in a demanding, high-stress world. They are energized by the fast-paced working style, the demands of multitasking, and the excitement of stiff competition. But most managers can't keep up that pace for long without physical and emotional consequences. The most successful managers tend to be those who prioritize their tasks, delegate responsibilities, and know when to leave their work problems behind them.

How can I tell whether my worry is productive or toxic?

It's important to tell the difference between positive stress and toxic worry. If you feel good about what you're doing, if you're producing excellent work on time and under budget, then enjoy yourself! But if you're worried and anxious, unable to concentrate on your work, or unhappy about even going to work, then the stress you feel is poisoning your life—at work and at home.

What are some of the signs of toxic stress?

Some signs of toxic stress are subtle and difficult to detect, while others are clearly recognizable. The most common indicators are changes in behavior such as decreased productivity, creativity, motivation, or confidence; increased irritability, fatigue, or pessimism; increased use of alcohol or other drugs; and increased physical ailments with no apparent cause. In practical terms, you may be dealing with a toxic level of stress if you find yourself canceling appointments, failing in an interview, or refusing to fly on an airplane just because you're too anxious.

Why is it important to talk with someone about the problem?

One of the first rules for managing stress is *never worry alone.*

Talk with someone you trust. Why? Talking helps you feel more in control because it lets you know you're not alone—you're sharing the burden with another person. Your talking partner can ease your mind by reassuring you that you're okay or that the problem can be solved. He or she may also help you reflect on the situation and get the facts straight. When you're stressed, you tend to exaggerate the situation, making it worse in your mind. A talking partner can offer a different point of view—a different way of seeing the situation.

How do deep-breathing exercises help manage stressful moments?

Deep breathing can help in several ways. First, the very act of taking a deep breath helps you relax—it slows the heart rate and the respiratory rate, and it keeps the pH level of the blood stable. Just *noticing* your breathing takes your mind off the problem and puts it onto your body. Also, many people tend to hold their breath when stressed—deep breathing forces them to get oxygen back into their systems.

To Learn More

Notes and articles

Cohen, Sacha. "De-Stress for Success." *Training & Development* (November 1997).

> This article provides practical ideas for reducing stress in the workplace, for example, how to improve the quality of your work environment, how to control information overload, and how to give your body a break.

Gary, Loren. "Fighting the Enemy Within." *Harvard Management Update* (February 2002).

> In the uncertainty and gloom of a recession, employees naturally worry that they'll be included in the next round of layoffs. And, anxious to secure the necessary financial and human resources for their key projects, managers have to fight to keep their units intact. In such an environment, it's no wonder that negative office politics are intensified. Although you can't expect to root politics out completely, the advice given in this article is intended to help you head off the game playing instead of teaching you how to play.

Harvard Business School Publishing. "How to Get People on Board." *Harvard Management Update* (June 2000).

This article takes a leader's point of view in helping employees cope with change, shows managers how to identify sources of anxiety, and describes what managers can do to facilitate the process of change.

Laabs, Jennifer. "Overload: What's Causing It, and How to Solve It." *Workforce* (January 1999).

In this useful article, Laabs gives managers ideas for helping their direct reports avoid or manage work overload. She also points out that in order to help your team become more productive, you must first understand the cause of excess work and then work to resolve the situation.

Books

Benson, Herbert. *The Relaxation Response.* New York: Avon Books, 2000.

In an updated and expanded version of this best-selling classic, Benson describes the physiological basis of the relaxation response and its benefits in counteracting the negative effects of stress; he then takes readers through detailed steps to achieve this state of relaxation.

Breier, Mark. *The 10-Second Internet Manager.* New York: Random House, 2000.

As suggested by the title, this book provides many practical, quick tips for coping with the Internet age. For example, his advice on dealing with e-mail—often overwhelming in today's workplace—is right to the point: "Delete, divert, delay, or deal with it," but make the decision immediately.

Hallowell, Edward M. *Connect*. New York: Pantheon Books, 1999.

The most recent book by this topic's expert, *Connect* describes twelve important ways we can make connections with our families, friends, colleagues, activities, ideas, and ourselves! A tremendously important guide for dealing with the human issues of loneliness and alienation—both in the workplace and beyond.

Hallowell, Edward M. *Worry*. New York: Ballantine Books, 1997.

The title of this book says it all—here Dr. Hallowell takes a wide and deep look at worry and offers tips, guides, and programs for dealing with the toxic worry so many of us struggle with in today's hectic and stressful world.

Other learning source

www.drhallowell.com

Go to this Web site to find out more about this topic's subject matter expert, Dr. Edward Hallowell, his newsletter, and the Hallowell Center.

Sources

We would like to acknowledge the sources who aided in developing this topic.

Benson, Herbert. *The Relaxation Response.* New York: Avon Books, 2000.

———. "Your Innate Asset for Combating Stress." *Harvard Business Review* (July-August 1974).

———, and Eileen M. Stuart. *The Wellness Book: The Comprehensive Guide to Maintaining Health and Treating Stress-Related Illness.* New York: Simon & Schuster, 1993.

Berman, Mark L. "Avoiding Burnout through Personal Energy Management." *American Society for Training and Development* (February 1995).

Cohen, Sacha. "De-Stress for Success." *Training & Development* (November 1997).

Davidson, Jeff. "Avoiding Job Burnout," an online program at www.youachieve.com.

Friedman, Stewart D., Perry Christensen, and Jessica DeGroot. "Work and Life: The End of the Zero-Sum Game." *Harvard Business Review* (November-December 1998).

Hallowell, Edward M. Personal conversations with author, October 2000.

———. *Connect.* New York: Pantheon Books, 1999.

———. *Worry.* New York: Ballantine Books, 1997.

Harvard Management Update editors. "How to Get People on Board." *Harvard Management Update* (June 2000).

Laabs, Jennifer. "Overload: What's Causing It, and How to Solve It." *Workforce* (January 1999).

Rosenthal, David S., and Kenneth L. Minaker. *Stress Management Guidebook.* Harvard University Health Services Good Health Management Series. Cambridge, MA: Harvard University Health Services, 1996.

Tools and Resources for Managing Your Time

This sample chart shows the results of a time audit, including the percentage breakdown shown in the bottom row.

BASELINE TIME-MANAGEMENT AUDIT TOOL

Week Ending:	Activity:	Activity:	Activity:	Activity:	Total Time/Day:
Monday					
Tuesday					
Wednesday					
Thursday					
Friday					
Total Time/ Activity					
% of Time					

TIME-LEVERAGING PLAN TOOL

Week

Goal-related Category	What does success look like? How will I know if I am successful?	% Time Required	Hours/ Workweek	Key Activities

TIME-BOX TOOL

Adapt this to any type of calendar or software program

Schedule, Week of _____

Time	Monday	Tuesday	Wednesday
8:00 a.m.	Task: Actual time spent:	Task: Actual time spent:	Task: Actual time spent:
9:00 a.m.	Task: Actual time spent:	Task: Actual time spent:	Task: Actual time spent:
10:00 a.m.	Task: Actual time spent:	Task: Actual time spent:	Task: Actual time spent:
11:00 a.m.	Task: Actual time spent:	Task: Actual time spent:	Task: Actual time spent:
12:00 p.m.	Task: Actual time spent:	Task: Actual time spent:	Task: Actual time spent:
1:00 p.m.	Task: Actual time spent:	Task: Actual time spent:	Task: Actual time spent:
2:00 p.m.	Task: Actual time spent:	Task: Actual time spent:	Task: Actual time spent:

Notes:

OFFICE SPACE SHOPPING LIST TOOL

**Keep receipts and leave factory labels on containers
until you are sure you want to keep them.**

Category/Item Type	Container	Space Needed
Bills to be paid	Plastic drawer Other:	
Must-do today	Open-top bin Other:	
Have-to-do soon	Closed-top bin Other:	
To file	Open-top bin Other:	
Reading materials—journals, newsletters, etc.	Magazine holders Other:	
Magazines	Magazine rack Tote bag Other:	
Price lists and catalogs	Closed-top bins Magazine holders Other:	
Outgoing items	Bin Other:	
Papers for projects	Document box Size: Other:	
Instruction manuals and warranties	Plastic, closed-top container Other:	
Small items, pens, pencils, stickies, paper clips, etc.		
CDs	CD notebook CD shelf CD box Other:	
Shelves	Dimensions:	

CHECKLIST FOR EVALUATING YOUR SCHEDULE

	Always	Often	Sometimes	Never
Are you making measurable progress on achieving your goals?				
Do you feel more prepared and focused?				
Are you completing the tasks you set for the week?				
Do you have realistic plans for completing tasks you have not finished?				
Are you scheduling approximately the right number of activities?				
Are your time estimates becoming more accurate?				
Can you reduce any activities or tasks that do not support your high-priority tasks?				

Frequently Asked Questions

What's the biggest problem new managers face in managing their time?

You cannot successfully manage your time if you don't know *how* you should be spending it. The biggest problem new managers face is understanding their goals and priorities. They are not really sure what they should be doing. Because of this uncertainty, new managers often spend time working on the wrong things or let others pull them into activities that aren't directly tied to their priorities and goals. To better understand how you should be spending your time, work with your supervisor to clarify expectations and responsibilities. At the same time, start to get a handle on how long your new responsibilities take so you can better estimate and plan your time as you grow in your new role.

Does it ever make sense to delay important tasks?

It often makes sense to delay working on a task until you have key information or resources. It is also often best not to work on jobs that require sensitivity and clarity of thought when you are upset, angry, or tired. Just make sure that your impulse to delay an important task is not a form of procrastinating.

How do I learn to say no?

Once you've established clear priorities and created a schedule, saying no will become easier. You can set boundaries by explaining your priorities. Rather than putting out fires all day long, schedule a block of time each day to handle issues presented by your direct reports. Then defer all requests but emergencies to that time block. Become disciplined about running meetings, and train reports to recognize issues that can wait until meetings, so they can bring them up then.

Saying no to management can be a little trickier, but you can still use the same techniques. Clearly explain your priorities and the importance of your schedule. You can't always say no when you want to, but if you are firm about boundaries, those times will be less frequent.

What if it is impossible to estimate how long something will take?

Typically difficulties with estimates result from lack of experience with a given task. Regardless of the task, a certain level of time management and estimation needs to be applied to control the costs from becoming unfeasible. Some tasks, such as hiring the right person or following creative pursuits, might seem impossible to estimate, but start by breaking the task down using best guesses. Guess how many people you will need to interview and how long each interview will take. Factor in other time on the pursuit, such as time spent checking references, reviewing résumés, rewriting a job description, and so on. Once you break down a task into its component parts, estimating the total time required will become more obvious.

Another way to estimate a task that you may be unfamiliar with is to ask for help. Find a coworker who is knowledgeable about the job and ask for advice.

The better you become at estimating, the more likely you will be satisfied by your ability to accomplish your goals in the time you set for yourself.

I always forget my initial priorities because I get caught up in the day-to-day matters. How can I avoid this?

Sticking to your priorities is typically a matter of discipline more than anything else. If others constantly interrupt you, you need to lay down some ground rules—ask for no interruptions during a *"closed-door quiet time."* If there is simply not enough time in the day, you need to review your time allocations with your manager and find an alternative solution. A common problem is that you simply have too much to do.

What should I do if I'm spending too much time on something I'm not very good at?

It depends. It's always more comfortable to work on things you are good at, but don't neglect your weaknesses completely. The key is to identify those weaknesses that are inhibiting your growth or success and work on them. For example, a middle-aged sales representative who is uncomfortable with technology will probably have to buckle down and learn how to use a computer in order to stay current.

On the other hand, spending too much time on weak areas that you are not motivated to strengthen or that are not standing in your way can be frustrating and a waste of time. In these cases, you are better off figuring out a *"work-around plan"* and getting back to leveraging your strengths. You will need to judge whether the activities are the ones you want to spend time developing skills for yourself, or whether you need to delegate them.

Test Yourself

How well do you understand the principles of time-leveraging and time-management?

1. In time-leveraging, what is the driving factor in how you use your time?

    a. The goals of your organization.

    b. Your own most important goals.

    c. Your schedule.

2. You know you are spending too much time on a particular activity and want to make a case to your supervisor for additional resources. In addition to your job description, what else will you use?

    a. Your performance appraisal.

    b. The job description of people to whom you want to delegate.

    c. The results of a time audit.

3. What is the first step in creating a time-management plan?

    a. Break important goals into activities with time estimates.

    b. Create a schedule.

    c. Write to-do lists.

4. How can anyone become more and more effective at scheduling their time?

   a. Keep track of actual time spent on tasks.

   b. Use software programs developed for scheduling.

   c. Reduce time-wasting activities.

5. One way to reduce time spent on low-priority activities is to delegate. Which of the following should almost never be a part of delegating a task?

   a. Giving clear expectations of results.

   b. Granting authority to get the job done.

   c. Ensuring that a precise process for achieving results is followed.

6. Someone comes into your office with a fairly complicated but nonurgent matter that needs input from others on your team. What would be an effective way to handle this interruption?

   a. Make it clear that you are busy and can't talk now.

   b. Ask to defer the discussion to the weekly team meeting.

   c. Call other team members who are involved and have a quick, stand-up meeting to resolve the problem as quickly as possible.

7. Your desk is piled high with all kinds of papers—mail, project information, snapshots, bids, bills. You spend lots of time going through the mess and it's frustrating. Of the following, which is the best way to start getting organized?

a. Throw nonessential items away.

b. Create a pile of the most important things you need to do now.

c. Clear off your desk completely and clean it.

8. What's an effective way to approach completing a task that you don't want to do?

a. Promise yourself a reward after the task is completed.

b. Plan to spend as little time on it as possible.

c. Schedule it for another time.

9. What's an effective way to solve the phone-tag problem?

a. Be persistent. Keep calling back and eventually you will contact the person.

b. Call people in the evening at home.

c. Use e-mail to schedule phone conversations.

10. What's an effective way to handle paperwork?

a. Sort the paperwork into piles of highest priority, medium priority, and lowest priority.

b. Always reply right on the paper received rather than create a separate reply.

c. Try to handle any paper document only once.

Answers to test questions

1b. The time you have is yours to spend, and your own goals, both personal and professional, should drive how you spend it. A clear understanding of what your goals really are will help you leverage your time.

2c. Your job description, combined with the results of a one-week audit showing how you actually spend your time, can make a compelling case for you to get additional resources, or at least re-define your role.

3a. Before you can create an effective schedule or to-do list, you need to determine what activities will help you reach your goals and estimate how much time these activities will take.

4a. As you become better at estimating how long various tasks and activities take, you can create more realistic schedules. By sticking to realistic schedules, you can manage your own expectations about your goals and your progress toward them.

5c. When you delegate, focus on results, not process. People need the latitude to achieve desired results in the way that is most effective for them.

6b. Make team meetings more useful by deferring important but nonurgent issues to them. Over time, team members will begin to use the team meeting more effectively themselves. Simply kicking the person out may be rude, and having an immediate meeting with other members is disruptive to everyone's schedule.

7c. Being disorganized is frustrating and wastes time. Simply throwing things away or creating an in-box pile won't help you solve your problem. Clear off your desk and create a storage plan so you can start to make your office space work for you.

8a. Promising yourself a reward, such as taking a walk or a coffee break after completing something you'd like to avoid, can help you accomplish things you don't like doing and make the job more enjoyable. If you rush through the task, you may not do it correctly. Scheduling for another time is also known as procrastinating.

9c. Persistence may help you get through to people, but phone tag is still a real time-waster for many people. Many people use e-mail to schedule phone conversations. E-mail can also be used to inform people of what the conversation will be about, so the conversation will be as useful as possible.

10c. Try to handle paper only once. Paper pileup can be overwhelming. Have a place to put every piece of paper that comes into your hands, for example a trashcan, an in-box, a magazine rack, an out-box, a catalog storage container.

To Learn More

Notes and Articles

Jim Billington. "Fairly Timeless Insights on How to Manage Your Time." *Harvard Management Update*, February 1997.

Too much literature on time management stresses how to do more faster—essentially how to manage a to-do list. Instead, managers should visualize the end result by "getting on the balcony—seeing the whole field of play and where their undertaking should fit in." Only work that is truly necessary should be done, and the addiction to urgency—fighting fires, fielding calls, firing off memos, and attending irrelevant meetings that can consume a manager's day but add little lasting value—should be avoided. The goal of enlightened time management is to allow people to spend most of their time on work that is truly important, but relatively nonurgent. Work and leisure should both be governed by this same philosophy, because by balancing excellence in work with excellence in relaxation, our lives become healthier and a great deal more creative. A short checklist of practical tips to increase efficiency is included.

John P. Kotter. "What Effective General Managers Really Do."
Harvard Business Review OnPoint Enhanced Edition. Boston:
Harvard Business School Publishing, 2000.

> Controlling your time and highly structuring your sched-
> ule can help you boost your efficiency and productivity.
> But, as Kotter explains, going *too* far in that direction can
> actually hinder your effectiveness. Managers who limit
> their interactions to orderly, focused meetings actually
> shut themselves off from vital information and relation-
> ships. Kotter shows how seemingly wasteful activities like
> chatting in hallways and having impromptu conversations
> and gatherings can in fact be remarkably efficient. The key
> to taking advantage of these opportunities? Develop flexi-
> ble agendas and broad relationship networks. Be willing to
> respond opportunistically to the events around you—but
> within a clear framework that guides your decisions.

Hal Lancaster. "Time Management Takes Planning in the Real
World." *Wall Street Journal*, August 19, 1997.

> This article examines why traditional time-management
> systems have failed. The author describes how many tradi-
> tional systems do not take into consideration real-world
> obstacles. He compiles his own list of obstacles and possi-
> ble solutions.

Dwight Moore. "Managing Message Overload." *Harvard Management Update*, November 1999.

> Getting swamped by a deluge of communications? Moore,
> an industrial psychologist, explains how to rearrange your

priorities and more effectively manage the many messages that come your way during a typical workday.

William Oncken, Jr., and Donald L. Wass. "Management Time: Who's Got the Monkey?" *Harvard Business Review* OnPoint Enhanced Edition. Boston: Harvard Business School Publishing, 2000.

Many managers feel overwhelmed. They have too many problems—too many monkeys—on their backs. All too often, they find themselves running out of time while their subordinates are running out of work. Such is the common phenomenon described by the late William Oncken, Jr., and Donald L. Wass in this 1974 HBR classic. This article describes how the manager can reverse this phenomenon and delegate effectively. In his accompanying commentary, Stephen R. Covey discusses both the enduring power of this message and how theories of time management have progressed beyond these ideas.

Thomas J. Peters. "Leadership: Sad Facts and Silver Linings." *Harvard Business Review* OnPoint Enhanced Edition. Boston: Harvard Business School Publishing, 2001.

Peters suggests that the "sad facts" of managerial life can be turned into opportunities to communicate values and to persuade. The fragmented nature of the executive's workday can also create a succession of opportunities to tackle bits of the issue stream. The fragmentation is precisely what permits a manager to fine-tune, test, and retest the strategic signals being sent to the company.

Peters suggests that the leader must become adept at controlling the process by nudging it in the desired direction.

Kirsten D. Sandberg. "The Case for Slack: Building 'Incubation Time' into Your Week." *Harvard Management Update*, June 2001.

Companies are constantly striving to cut the slack time in their processes. But this zeal for lean operations has led many companies to cut the slack, or thinking time, out of human processes as well. In an era of tight production deadlines—and even tighter margins—how can you be sure to build in the "down time" workers at your company need to generate breakthrough ideas and strategies? Real-world managers and several academics discuss the merits of slack time and offer advice on how to fit this new essential into your business.

David Stauffer. "Making Sense of Your Time Bind, and Escaping It." *Harvard Management Update*, August 1997.

The author focuses on ways to manage the time bind. Using current research, he identifies specific tips for approaching time, setting goals, and scheduling time.

Constantine Von Hoffman. "Getting Organized." *Harvard Management Update*, January 1998.

Although there is no single best method for organizing yourself, this article taps into some perennially useful techniques for managing your disorganization. Through space management, organizing your schedule in collaboration with others, prioritizing your to-do list, and correctly filing things so they remain accessible, managers can reduce the hundreds of hours lost each year searching for lost items.

Books

Jack D. Ferner. *Successful Time Management: A Self-Teaching Guide*. New York: John Wiley & Sons, 1995.

This book provides a broad overview of the principles of time management. The author maintains that time management is a process that involves analysis, planning, and commitment. He includes exercises and references that can be incorporated into everyday professional and personal situations to help you manage your time successfully.

Julie Morgenstern. *Time Management from the Inside Out: The Foolproof System for Taking Control of Your Schedule and Your Life*. New York: Henry Holt, 2000.

Those who fear "time management" because they worry about living uncreative or overly scheduled lives will find themselves reassured by Morgenstern's ability to customize her system. The most important thing readers must do, she emphasizes, is to create a time-management system that fits one's personal style—whether it be spontaneous and easily distracted or highly regimented and efficient.

William Oncken, Jr., Hal Burrows, Kenneth Blanchard. *The One Minute Manager Meets the Monkey.* Quill, 1991.

The message in this book is let your direct reports take on the tasks they can and should do. Trust them and train them, but don't do it yourself!

Sources

We would like to acknowledge the sources that aided in developing this topic.

Elaine Biech, *The Consultant's Quick Start Guide*

Sandy Block, the Clutter Cutter

Beth Chapman, engagement manager, Health Care Consulting Services Group, McKesson Corp.

Elisabeth Choi, equity analyst

Melissa Raffoni, Managing Director, Professional Skills Alliance, Boston, Massachusetts

Michael Rothman, software developer

Peter and Laura Wakeman, owners, Great Harvest Bread Company

Stephen R. Covey, Roger Merrill, and Rebecca R. Merill. *First Things First: To Live, to Love, to Learn, to Leave a Legacy.* New York: Simon & Schuster, 1995.

William Oncken, Jr. *Managing Management Time: Who's Got the Monkey?* New York: Prentice Hall Trade, 1987.

Jim Temme. *Productivity Power: 250 Great Ideas for Being More Productive.* Mission, KS: SkillPath Publications, Inc., 1993.

Alex MacKenzie. *The Time Trap.* New York: AMACOM, 1997.

Melissa Raffoni. "Got a Need for Speed? What You Can Learn from Rapid Application Development." *Harvard Management Update*, November 2000.

Melissa Raffoni. "How to Be Sure You're Spending Your Time in the Right Places." *Harvard Management Update*, October 2001.

About the Subject Experts

James Waldroop and Timothy Butler, Subject Experts,
Shaping Your Career

Drs. James Waldroop and Timothy Butler are business career psychologists who worked together for almost twenty years at the Harvard Business School. Dr. Butler is now Senior Fellow and Director of Career Development at the Harvard Business School. They have spent many years helping businesspeople work through the career planning and development processes. Their online business career assessment tool, CareerLeader, is used by more than 400 universities and corporations around the world. (For more information, go to www.careerleader.com.)

They are also the authors of four highly acclaimed *Harvard Business Review* articles as well as three books: *Getting Unstuck: How Dead Ends Become New Paths, Maximum Success: Changing the Twelve Behavior Patterns That Keep You from Getting Ahead,* and *Discovering Your Career in Business.* They are frequent contributors to the national media, with articles in *Fortune* and *Fast Company,* and have appeared on radio and TV to discuss issues related to managing your career, retaining talent, and maximizing personal effectiveness.

Dr. Edward Hallowell, Subject Expert, Managing Stress

Dr. Edward Hallowell has been an instructor at Harvard Medical School and the founder of the Hallowell Center for Cognitive and Emotional Health in Sudbury and Andover, MA. Dr. Hallowell is a recognized expert on the topics of worry and stress, its causes and cures. He frequently appears in the national news media and on shows such as *Oprah, 20/20, The Today Show,* and *Good Morning America.* He is the author of several best-selling books, including his recent releases, *Dare to Forgive, Connect: 12 Vital Ties That Open Your Heart, Lengthen Your Life and Deepen Your Soul,* and *Worry: Hope and Help for a Common Problem.* You can find out more about Dr. Hallowell and his work at his Web site: www.drhallowell.com.

Melissa Raffoni, Subject Expert, Managing Time

Melissa Raffoni is Founder of Professional Skills Alliance. She has over ten years of professional experience, working with hundreds of clients ranging from start-up to Fortune 500, with a significant focus on business-to-business services. Prior to starting her independent consulting practice, Melissa played significant roles building Oracle's Change Performance Consulting Practice and *Inc. Magazine*'s Eagles CEO Peer Group Program. She is on the faculty at the Sloan School of Management at MIT and has published numerous articles with *Harvard Management Update.*